HUSTLE AND A
HIGHER PURPOSE
THE PHOENIX IN ME

To everyone still in the fire.

May this book be a spark, a mirror, or a reminder — that rising is still possible.

And to **Brock Felt** — you were the messenger sent to plant the seed. I didn't know it then, but telling my story would become part of my legacy... and my higher purpose. Thank you.

Contents

Chapter 1

<u>Born in the Fire</u>

phoenix (noun) 1. A mythical bird that cyclically burns to ashes and is reborn, rising renewed from its own destruction. 2. A symbol of transformation, resilience, and rebirth after hardship.

Phoenix, AZ — Maryvale. Where I learned how to hustle before I learned how to crawl.

I was born and raised in Phoenix, Arizona — Westside, Maryvale to be exact. Back then, I didn't think much about what kind of neighborhood it was. It was just home. But looking back, I realize now it wasn't the safest or the easiest place to grow up.

I was raised by a single mom doing her best with what little we had. She already had my older brother, five years ahead of me, and later had my little sister, five years behind me. Three kids, three different dads, none of them stuck around. The only checks coming in were AFDC and food stamps, but somehow, she kept us fed and together. We didn't grow up spoiled — not even close — but we grew up real.

I didn't grow up thinking my life was hard — it just was. I wasn't walking around feeling sorry for myself. I wasn't an unhappy kid. Sure, I didn't have the latest video games or get to play on the organized sports teams like some of the other kids. I wasn't rocking Jordans — I was lucky to have shoes that held up through the school year. But I wasn't bitter about it. I accepted life for what it was.

2

I've always been book smart. In second grade, I even got tested for the gifted program. I didn't pass, but not many kids did back then — the criteria was tougher than it is now. Still, I always knew I had something in me. I wasn't sure what it meant yet, but I felt it.

I don't know if I'd call it "survival mode," but I knew early on that if I wanted more out of life, I was going to have to go get it myself. Nobody was handing out opportunities where I came from. My mom did her best, but the truth was, we just didn't have much — and if I was gonna break out of that cycle, I couldn't just wait around. I had to move different. Think different. Hustle for mine.

Music was always in me. From a young age, I was drawn to gangster rap — something about it spoke to the way I saw the world. It wasn't just entertainment; it was a reflection of what I was seeing around me. I'd listen to artists who told stories that sounded like the lives of people I knew. Same with the movies — Boyz n the Hood, Menace II Society — they didn't feel like fiction to me. They felt like a mirror.

With that influence and my surroundings being what they were — and watching my older brother start drifting in that same direction — I guess it was inevitable. When you're raised around it, it doesn't feel like you're choosing a path. It just feels like that's the path already there.

I'd been through a lot in my life. Started selling drugs when I was 13 — crystal meth and weed at first. By 14, I caught my first real case: armed robbery, aggravated assault, and kidnapping. And no, it wasn't a child we kidnapped — it was a grown man. But they don't care how they word it. I remember that detective coming in and laying it all out. I thought I was never going home. I knew I did wrong, and I remember looking my mom in the eye and promising her I was done. That I'd change.

But the moment I walked out those doors, it was like the streets called me back. House arrest didn't slow me down — I was selling weed, stacking money. Then at 16, I caught another armed robbery and kidnapping charge for hitting a crack house. They tried to charge me as an adult. I sat for close to six months, and eventually, they dropped it without prejudice. I turned 17 right after that and tried to bounce back.

Then three days after Christmas, I got shot. Took one in the chest and in the arm. Bullet shattered my arm, collapsed my lung. The bullet is still stuck in my back — too close to the spine to remove. You'd think something like that would make you slow down. But it didn't. I kept gangbanging, hustling, chasing money. I wasn't some corner boy, though — I was always trying to be on the wholesale side of things. Heavy into weed, then I got deeper into selling crack.

At 19, I got raided because of my roommate. That led to a federal gun case at 20 — the ATF hit me for fully automatics and silencers. I ended up signing for 37–46 months. Even that didn't break me.

Even having kids didn't slow me down either. I always handled my responsibilities — I wasn't out here high or strung out. I smoked a little weed when I was younger, drank a little, that's it. But mentally and spiritually, I was still in the same place. I wasn't religious. God wasn't gonna save me — I didn't believe in that.

Eventually though... I just got tired. Tired of the energy. Tired of always being drained. Constant drama, fights with my kids' mom, depression sneaking in like a thief at night. It wasn't just about me anymore — my family deserved better. I deserved better. That's when I started looking into things like "energy vampires." That's what led me to a different kind of path

— not religion, but something spiritual. I started learning to be thankful, to accept things I couldn't change. Especially the past.

I don't know exactly what it is — I can't fully explain it. But there's always been something inside me, something that wouldn't let me quit. I've been knocked down, hit walls, faced charges, bullets, betrayals, depression — but I keep getting back up. And somehow, things always fall into place. Not perfect. Not easy. But just enough to keep going.

I stopped acting like I had all the answers. These days, I'm more open-minded. I pay attention to my mental and physical health. I try to experience new things — good things. I work on rejecting negativity and staying mindful of what I feed my brain. The movies I watch, the music I listen to, the energy I allow in — it all matters.

I'm still here for a reason. I don't take that lightly anymore.

Chapter 2

<u>This Was Just Normal</u>

trauma (noun) 1. A deeply distressing or disturbing experience. 2. A lasting emotional wound caused by overwhelming stress, often invisible to the outside world.

Sometimes, trauma doesn't feel like trauma when it's all you've ever known.

Maryvale -- where the streets were cracked and the homes were humble. Even with as little as we had, I didn't see it as poor. It was just life. My mom was raising three kids. I was the middle child -- That five-year spread both ways gave me a unique seat in the house -- close enough to watch, far enough to keep some space.

Some of my earliest memories are a blur of love and trauma. I remember one day my brother scooping me up and running me across the street while my mom and her boyfriend at the time were in a violent domestic fight. I was just a kid, but I knew it wasn't right -- I knew we needed help. Another memory -- my mom visiting a man who was locked up he ended up being like a stepdad to me. I didn't know the full story at the time; I just remember prison gates, visiting rooms and my Hot Wheels not passing through the metal detectors.

I also remember the good -- being dropped off at my grandparents' liquor store where they lived in the back. When they sold that store, they bought an RV and took me and my brother fishing, traveling all over the western U.S. for a couple of summers. There were peaceful moments too -- running home from school just to catch cartoons, getting lost in my own world playing with my toys. Sometimes I was so quiet, it was like I disappeared into myself.

Our house was a mix. My mom loved us -- that was never in question -- but life was stressful. I remember when she fell into a coma just after she had my sister and we found out she was diabetic. That shook the whole family. Me and my brother used to get into full-blown fistfights as kids, but I also knew no matter what, if someone messed with me, he had my back.

The neighborhood was wild, but it didn't feel wild to me. It was just normal. I remember seeing my mom stashing money in a curtain rod keeping a nest egg for when my stepdad would leave, he never stuck around for long periods of time. I didn't realize until later that what I saw -- drug use, alcoholism, domestic violence, people barely holding it together -- wasn't everyone's normal. I saw people nodding off, people fighting in the streets, people crying and cussing in the middle of the night. My stepdad used to spend hours in the bathroom. I didn't understand it back then, but later I found out he was shooting heroin. We had burn marks on the couch and blankets from cigarettes -- signs of the chaos nobody talked about.

When it came to role models, it all depended on my age. I had sports heroes like Bo Jackson and Larry Johnson, but the people I really absorbed game from were rappers and street legends. Eazy-E, Dr. Dre, Snoop Dogg, Spice 1 -- they were speaking my language before I even understood what the words meant. And then there was my brother and his friends. If he was stealing car stereos at 15, I was out jacking whole cars with the driver still in it at gunpoint by the time I got to his age. That was the evolution -- not in a good way, but in the only way I knew.

Even with everything going on, I didn't feel different from other kids -- not at first. I had friends I played video games with; kids I shot hoops with after school. I wasn't walking around thinking, "My life is harder." It was just my life. I never wanted to see those kids fall into the things I fell into. Just like with my own kids now -- I never wanted them to go down the same path. I didn't know how to avoid the street, but I knew I didn't want to see them in it.

Back then, I didn't know what trauma was. I didn't know what healing meant. I didn't have words like "cycles" or "generational wounds." All I knew was that I had to survive -- and I had to do it on my own terms.

Chapter 3

Getting Deeper Into the Flame

initiation (noun) 1. The action of beginning something. 2. A ceremony or process that marks entry into a new role, group, or stage of life often with trials or sacrifices.

Some people try to run from the fire. I kept walking toward it. Not because I loved the heat... but because I didn't know anything else.

By the time I was 13, I wasn't just watching the streets -- I was in them. It wasn't a sudden turning point or dramatic moment. It felt more like a slow, steady walk deeper into the fire. One step led to the next, and before I realized it, I was living the life I had been observing for years. There was no roadmap, no big aha moment -- just a progression that felt natural at the time.

I had been trying to get in the game for a minute. I didn't have any money, no real plug. I was just a kid trying to get a front. I remember this one kid at school who acted like he had it like that -- kept stringing me along, saying he forgot the sack, saying he'd bring it the next day. Eventually, I pushed him to take me to his apartment, and that's when he tried to give me oregano, telling me it was weed like I wouldn't know the difference. That was my first lesson in the game: people will test you, especially when you're new and hungry.

But I kept at it, and I finally caught a real break middle-manning a deal for some crystal -- the old kind, not that glass they started calling it later. It was with some Cubans who stayed in these apartments I used to hang out at. They didn't speak much English, but we found a way to communicate through hustle. That first play made me feel like I had finally accomplished something. It wasn't about the money -- it was about being in. It felt like validation.

The hustle didn't explode overnight, though. I wasn't some young king-pin. I had to figure it out as I went. I put what I made into weed, trying to build something. The Cubans, meanwhile, started trying to get fronts from me, always saying they'd pay later. One of them ended up shooting someone or something, and just like that, they disappeared from the spot -- still owing me money. I had already jumped into another hustle by then, so I just charged it to the game. Another lesson.

All this while, I was still going to school. 8th grade. I showed up every day, and at first the teachers were proud. I had been a handful in 7th -- always ditching, always in trouble -- so they were surprised to see me trying. But that didn't last long. I got into a fight midway through the year and got sent to in-school suspension again. Eventually, they just gave me my diploma and were done with me. I wasn't failing because I wasn't smart -- I was already mentally checked out. I had bigger plans.

At home, I kept everything low-key. I didn't want to bring any drama to my mom. She already had enough to deal with. My brother had a good plug at the time, but I hadn't involved him in anything -- until one day he found some rolled-up dimes of weed in my shoe. That was the moment. He didn't trip. In fact, it became a kind of unspoken support. He saw what I was doing and instead of trying to stop me, he stood by me -- like he always did.

That bond went back to when I was even younger. I remember giving myself my first tattoo -- my initials -- on the inside of my leg with a needle and thread after watching my brother and his friends do it. I was in 4th grade, sleeping on the floor and somehow him and his friend noticed it, he didn't tell my mom. He was probably hiding his tattoos from her too, but I looked up to him. That influence was real, and now we were both in the life.

By the time I was 14, I was surrounded by gang members from different areas. I hadn't officially claimed anything yet, but I was affiliated. I hung around people from different hoods, but most my homies were from one in particular -- the one I would eventually get put on. I didn't get jumped in until I was 16, right after I got off house arrest, but mentally I had already made the choice.

Looking back now, I know exactly what pulled me in. It wasn't just money or power. It was belonging. It felt like being part of a team -- like having an identity. I wanted to represent something. I wanted people to know who I was, and what I stood for. When you're young belonging means the world, being known matters. And in that life, I finally felt officially in.

Chapter 4

<u>When the Streets Call You Back</u>

consequence (noun) 1. A result or effect of an action or condition. 2. The price of living a life where survival becomes normal.

The streets don't always take you out right away. Sometimes they wait until you think you're safe.

Getting jumped into the hood didn't really change much. I had already been reppin and running with the homies. It was just official now. But even then, my closest homeboys didn't want to do it — one pulled a gun out on the others mid-jump in because he didn't want them doing it. That's how close we were. But it still went down, and that was that.

By this time, I was in full hustle mode. I got kicked out of high school during the first week of my second year for trying to stab a kid with a pencil — he and some others were plotting to jump me. School was pretty much over after that. I did end up going to another high school for a little bit, but I ended up catching another firearm case. I only did about thirty days and it was dismissed, that was my 1st Christmas locked up. I went back to that same school one more time, I only had 2 classes Math and English, I didn't do much work. My English teacher put me on to the book Siddhartha and I actually read it, it stuck with me. Eventually I just dropped out though, but I wasn't trippin. I had my hustle...

Not long after my official jump-in, I caught an armed robbery case for hitting a crack house. I still don't know why the cops even came. We were leaving out the front when they were rushing in. I tried to escape out the back, but there was only one way in and out. Bars on the windows. Padlock on the back door. My crime partner Chico — he got away. Just bolted out the front. I can speak on it now — he's no longer with us, and the statute of limitations is up.

But me? I got stuck. Charged in adult court. Bond was $160,000 per count — wasn't going nowhere. They offered me a five-year plea deal. I didn't take it. Sat there fighting the case for almost six months, stressed out. Then they dismissed it. Just like that.

My girl couldn't hang, though. We broke up a couple months later. Yeah, I had thoughts of changing my life while I was inside, but they didn't last long. Only real experience I got out of it was a stay in one of Joe Arpaio's jails. Pink socks. Black and white stripes. A lunch sack we called a Ladmo bag. Jail full of gang members. Tension and animosity everywhere.

Once the case was dismissed, I went back to my mom's apartment, ready to bounce back. Cops left my car in front of the crack house — someone tried to steal it after I got arrested. The alarm kill switch was jacked, so I had to get that fixed. I had a strap at the house and sold it to get a quarter pound of weed to flip. But then I blew my re-up. Had to come up somehow — ended up jacking some rims.

Next day, when I went to go try and sell them, I got into it with some guys in traffic. That's when I got shot.

I took one in the chest and in the arm.

Crazy part — my mom was sick that day. I went to the store to get her some orange juice for her blood sugar. I never kissed her goodbye, but that day I did — kissed her on the forehead and told her I loved her. That would've been the last thing I ever said to her.

I had gotten back with my girl, too. Dropped her off, then picked up the homies. Five deep in the car. I was the only one who got hit. I didn't cry. My life didn't flash before my eyes. I thought I was a goner, I just accepted it.

The shooter pointed his gun right at me — middle of the day. I threw my hands up and said "what," but he didn't care — started bustin. The car behind them started firing too. Two cars deep. I ducked, but he caught me through the door.

All I could hear was the homies yelling, "Go! Go! Go!"

I realized I'd been hit. Tried to drive, but I couldn't. I threw the car in park in the middle of the intersection. Face — my homie — jumped out, ran around, scooted me over, and took the wheel. They were arguing where to take me — what hospital. I saw a payphone next to a Jack in the Box and told them, "Go call 911." Face jumped the curb and pulled up next to it. The other homies jumped out and ran for help.

They tried to pull me out of the car, but I told them just leave me alone. I was fading fast. Last thing I remember as they ended up pulling me out the car was looking up at Face.

They said I started speaking in tongues after I blacked out.

Next thing I know, I'm waking up. Oxygen mask on my face. Stripped down to my boxers. Being placed on a gurney. People asking me questions.

I wasn't scared. I was just mad. Mad that I got shot.

Chapter 5

Hard to Kill

resilience (noun) 1. The ability to withstand or recover quickly from difficult conditions. 2. The mental and emotional strength to keep going, even when the world expects you to break.

Some people wear scars. Others wear survival like armor.

I remember waking up being questioned, but I didn't know by who. Cops? Paramedics? They asked how old I was. I said 18. A minute later, they asked again, and I said 17. They called me out — "Why'd you lie?" I said, "I don't know. I'm f**kin shot! I don't know if I'm gonna get in trouble for this. How much is this gonna cost? My mom doesn't have money for this." I was mad. Mad I got shot. Mad I didn't know what was going to happen. I asked, "Where are my homies? I'm the only one who got shot? That motherf**ker shot me!" They said just keep talking to us as they proceeded to put me into the ambulance.

It's crazy — the whole time after I came to, the song "Walkin 2 My Funeral" by Brotha Lynch Hung was playing in my head. I went from accepting death to just wanting to survive. I told them, "Just keep me alive." They rushed me into St. Joseph's. Took me to the operating room. Told me they needed to cut open my left side — my lung had collapsed, and they had to drain the blood. I didn't care. I just wanted to live. I said, "Do what you gotta do." Every breath felt like being stabbed in the chest.

They did a CAT scan. I heard them talking about me maybe being paralyzed. I started kicking my feet like, Hell nah I can feel my legs. I ended up in ICU. Tubes in my nose, tubes down my throat.

Nurses trying to put a catheter in — I was like, "I'm good. We don't need that." My mom showed up mentally wrecked. My brother was locked up in county. She had no support. I can only imagine what she went through, especially now that I'm a parent.

The story made the news. I watched it from my ICU bed. Saw my homies on TV getting patted down — when we were the ones who got shot at. The homies showed up to the hospital too. Only two allowed in at a time. My girl came also.

They had to operate on my arm the next day. Rolled me into surgery. Put a mask on me, Told me to count backwards from ten. I only got to seven. Woke up with two metal plates and seventeen screws in my arm. Scar from my elbow to my upper arm. I stayed in the hospital a week. Spent New Year's in ICU, Face even called me at midnight to wish me a happy New Year. We had that kind of bond. I'll never forget that. Eventually, I got moved to a regular room. I was over it — tired of being there. Just wanted to go home. Had to get chest X-rays daily until I was cleared.

Finally, I got discharged. They told me to be careful not to get sick — my lung wasn't fully healed. So I stayed low-key at home for a couple months.

But nothing really changed.

I wasn't paranoid. I wasn't scared. I wasn't depressed. If anything, it brought me closer to my homies. Made me move different — shoot first, don't take chances. I even got a bulletproof vest. I felt invincible. Getting shot didn't slow me down. It sharpened me. Jail teaches you how to be a better criminal. Getting shot? It just made me more gangster.

I never realized all I put my mom through. Her first time seeing me in a cop car, I was 8. By 14, I caught an armed robbery case. At 16, a firearm case. Then another armed robbery. Fistfights with my brother. Now this — shot at 17. That's only up to that point. There was still more to come.

But yeah — getting shot? That was a badge, Especially back then. Not like today where every rapper's been shot. Back then, it meant something. And this wasn't a graze. I took one in the chest and the arm, survived it. I was proud. I felt hard to kill.

And my girl? I wasn't trippin on love. I was a teenager. I was more hyped to see my homies while I was in the hospital than her. She came. She was solid. But there was stuff between us. I had some resentment. She left me hanging before when I was locked up. It didn't bring us closer.

Looking back now, I don't have regrets. I see it all as part of the process. Even getting shot — I see it as a triumph. A survival story. If I could tell my 17-year-old self anything, it would be this: Just be more mindful of what you put your mom through. Your process is your process — but becoming the man you're meant to be is gonna take a toll on her. So do your best to treat her special. Show her the love she deserves.

Chapter 6

The Weight of Silence

disillusionment (noun) 1. A feeling of disappointment or discomfort when something you trusted or believed in starts to feel false.

Sometimes the silence says more than the truth ever will.

For the next month or so after getting shot, I was just chillin' recovering. Nothing specific stands out from that time. I wasn't in pain, I wasn't moving slower. I was just trying to figure out how to bounce back. Quiet days. No real plan. Just silence and survival.

Toward the end of February, I got the word something happened to my homeboy Carson. They said it was suicide, but that never sat right with me. He was out on bond, facing some time. We were both in county jail together charged as adults. He got bonded out not long after they dismissed my case. He was even locked up at the same time as I was back when I caught my first armed robbery too.

I didn't hear it from anyone directly. Nobody called, nobody pulled up. I wasn't around like that. I was still recovering. This was before social media. People didn't post every loss like they do now. I found out how a lot of us did back then — through the grapevine.

I guess I had been prepared for loss. Through the music I listened to and through the things I'd seen. It was just another badge. I was collecting them like a hood Boy Scout. Master P always had songs about his brother Kevin Miller getting killed —so it felt like it was just part of the life we were living. And as much as I didn't want to see any of my homies go, some part of me had been programmed to expect it. Maybe even weirdly looking forward to it.

Carson's death wasn't just a loss — it disrupted things. He was from California but had been back and forth to Phoenix, and he rode with us heavy. There were already tensions in the gang. Jealousy, division and now this. The ones who found him? People whispered about them. The story didn't feel right. I mean, who commits suicide with an assault rifle?

It shook the foundation. Made me question the code we thought we were living by.

I can't even remember exactly what I did next. But somehow, I got back in the game. I think my brother's old plug's daughter fronted me a quarter pound of weed. From there, I built everything back up. No dramatic comeback. Just the grind. Quiet, steady, and emotionless.

That's how it was. One moment you're trying to recover. The next, you're hearing about a funeral. Then, without even realizing it, you're back in motion like nothing ever happened.

Chapter 7

Shadows in the Same Colors

cycle (noun) 1. A series of events that are regularly repeated in the same order. 2. A trap disguised as routine.

The streets don't teach you how to escape the cycle — they teach you how to survive inside it.

Slowly, I started making my way back to the hood. There were different factions of my gang based on generation, who hung with who. We were all one, but the cracks were there. Come to find out, that's how most gangs are.

The original purpose of a gang was supposed to be protection — each other, the neighborhood — not graffiti, drugs, proving who's the hardest. The programming hit us through music and movies. As kids, it made sense. We didn't realize proving how hard we were could get us life in prison, and then we would just become stories or conversations. No letters, No money on the books just Forgotten. But I couldn't see that back then.

My crew was neutral. Other branches? Already in a civil war. I wasn't into banging like that. I didn't have many run-ins with rival gangs. I just wanted to get money. But I had my homies' backs.

I was doing alright. Mostly selling weed. This was before dispensaries and legal cannabis. Back then, it was all Reggie. Good pounds went for $500 — not the dirt brown, but good green Christmas bud. Break it down at $50 an Oz. and you'd profit $300 per pound. Push a pound a week and you were making more than someone with a 9 to 5. I even let half ounces go for $25. That made people feel like they were getting wholesale. That let me deal with fewer people, just the middlemen.

I can't remember what happened with my brother's old plug's daughter. I think she tried to raise the price or something. So I switched plugs — started working with a homegirl from my hood. The hustle kept growing. Stacked up enough to buy a new car. I wanted a Cutlass Supreme — typical gangster move — but I played it smarter. Picked up a little blue 4-door Cutlass Sierra. Still clean, but lowkey.

Then the losses started piling up.

One of the older homies — someone I didn't know well — overdosed or got a hotshot, died. Another homie a year or 2 younger than me, died in a car accident. That made three homies gone that year already.

My stepdad came back around. He'd been gone for a while but came into some inheritance or something. Cashed out a house for us — me, my mom, and my sister. Life looked good for a moment. My brother? He was already in prison, doing a three-piece if I remember right.

Then, near the end of the year — more death.

My homegirl, the one I was working with, doing good for herself, just bought a car and got a new apartment — got murdered. Another homegirl was with her, they shot her too. One more was in the bathroom, she survived. But again, speculation. People whispered it was folks from within the circle. Another betrayal, another silence.

That made five homies gone that year.

And then on the day after the anniversary of the day I got shot — another homeboy took himself out. Said he wasn't going back to prison. After a robbery he was running from the cops, and that was it.

That year was death in disguise. Money in one hand, mourning in the other. Life was looking good, but death was always just around the block.

Chapter 8

<u>No Plan B</u>

commitment (noun) 1. The state or quality of being dedicated to a cause, activity, or goal. 2. The moment you stop thinking about escape and only think about execution.

When I said I was all in, I meant it. There was no Plan B.

By the start of the new year, I was chasing more money. I got deeper into selling crack, still doing well with the weed. I was moving fearlessly, eyes wide open, always looking for new opportunity.

I was staying with my mom and stepdad at the time. My beeper stayed blowing up. Hustle all day, every day. Go to sleep, wake up, do it again. That was the cycle. That was the job.

I didn't have any doubts. I was fully in. This was what I was good at. And with the right plug, I knew I could've become a millionaire.

My relationship with my mom and stepdad was cool. They did their thing, I did mine. I didn't bring drama to the house. I handled my own food for the most part, didn't owe anything on the bills, and I wasn't home much anyway.

Then one day during the summer, it got hot. I was inside with two of my homies, just cooling off in the AC in the living room. Nothing wild, no disrespect. But my stepdad started trippin. I didn't like that. I appreciated having a roof over my head, but I didn't need to be somewhere I didn't feel wanted. So I bounced.

I stayed at Motel 6 for about a week, then got an apartment with my homeboy.

That move changed everything.

The hustle leveled up, I had more freedom. We landed a 2-bedroom apartment with utilities paid for — $613.87 a month. His sister hooked it up — said we worked for Reyes Construction or something like that. The property manager had worked at the last complex I lived at with my mom. They knew me. They looked out.

We split the rent — $300 each. That was nothing.

Every day we sat there, played video games, and hustled. That was life, no distractions, no plan b. Just the game and the grind.

Chapter 9

<u>Crossed Lines</u>

impulse (noun) 1. A sudden strong urge to act. 2. The split-second where emotion takes over logic.

In the streets, a second's reaction can write the next five years or more of your life.

The hustle was going great. I was networking, meeting new people. The apartment situation was solid — maybe that move was exactly what I needed in my process. Whatever got into my stepdad, it ended up pushing me out of my comfort zone, and that made me progress more.

But tension in the hood was high.

My crew, who had always been neutral, kind of ended up allying with another faction. That happened after I had a conflict with one of the other factions in the gang. I had sold a couple fools from the hood some crack. After that I had plans to go to a party with some homies and a couple homegirls. I picked my homies up, we stopped at the gas station and ran into some rivals from another hood. It got heated. There was an altercation.

Right after that, my car started messing up.

At the same time, the fools I had sold crack to from that other faction started blowing up my pager — fiending for more. I was dealing with the gas station drama, a broken car, and them blowing up my pager. They were salty, fiending. And just like that, they started looking for an excuse to have a problem with me. All of a sudden, it's beef with people from the same gang I'm in and supposed to be protected by.

I was always in the hood my girl lived there, them fools who wanted issues knew that. A few weeks later, they pulled up behind my car as I pulled up to my girls house. I'm slippin, my MAC-11 is in the trunk and I didn't have a belt on my pants. I get out the car, its three of them. I had 2 of my little homies, my girl and a homegirl with me. This fool Flaco tries to call me out, I tell them let me get a belt an we can run the heads up. One of them gives me his belt. I put it on. I take off my shirt, head to the middle of the road where we are gonna get down. Just as we get to the middle of the road Lil Chino's brother rolls by with a couple other homies. These fools get spooked run to their car and start cocking back guns and take off. I pop my trunk just in case, but them fools didn't come back. Word after that was be ready for whatever when we see each other.

One day after that I was cruising through the hood. I stopped at the homie's house, but he wasn't there. I'm about to head back to my apartment, and I spot that fool — the one with the issue. He's in a little blue Dodge. I spin the block, but he's gone. Took off.

The next morning I go back to the hood. I tell the homies, "That foo was riding through the block yesterday. Watch, I catch him again, that's on the gang — I'm busting at him."

And what do you know — as we walk out the door, one of the homies says, "Little blue Dodge like that?" I look. Yup, that's him.

The car stopped.

I pulled out my Glock and started poppin.

I'm thankful I missed now. But back then, I was trying to take that guy's life. Broad day. No second thoughts.

After that, I jumped in my ride and dipped. Neighbors were outside. Who knows who saw what, who wrote down my plate. I parked my car at my homie's grandma's house and caught a ride back to my apartment. I'd come back for the car when it felt safe.

I got home. Showered. Stayed lowkey.

But just in case the police came looking — I decided to dip out. Took my girl and hit the road. My first trip to Vegas on my own. I had cousins out there, and I had only been out there as a kid with my grandparents.

No plan. Just movement. Sometimes survival means relocation.

Chapter 10

<u>Running Ain't Peace</u>

escape (noun) A break from something dangerous, stressful, or
overwhelming. A fantasy that loses power the moment reality calls.

You can leave the city, but the hustle doesn't let go that easy.

I was 18. Nervous, but not scared. I had just shot at someone in broad
daylight and now I was heading to Vegas just in case the cops were looking
for me. I wasn't worried about gangsters — I could handle them. But jail?
I wasn't trying to go back. At the same time, it was kind of exciting. Me
and my girl pulled into town. I didn't even know where to stay. We found
a place — Pair-a-Dice Hotel. Then I got a hold of my cousin.

We liked it out there. Different energy, different pace. We even talked about
staying. So, we got a month-to-month furnished apartment off 13th and
Fremont. Talked about getting jobs, starting fresh. But those thoughts
didn't last. Vegas eventually became like a home away from home. We
stayed for a couple weeks, then went back to Phoenix. Then back to Vegas
again.

After that second trip, we gave up the apartment and returned to where
I already had everything built. Thankfully, my homeboy was holding it
down. He kept my weed moving. Kept my name strong. Because in this
game, if you're not available — you get replaced fast.

So just like that, we left peace behind. Back to the city. Back to the business.
Back to the hustle.

Chapter 11

Almost Got Me

close call (noun) 1. A moment where disaster was inches away. 2. The kind of silence that makes you rethink everything.

That day, I got lucky. But luck isn't a strategy.

The hustle has always been in me. Even when I was a kid, I'd hit the swap meet and flip sports cards. It came natural. Like it was my God-given talent. I was okay at a lot of things — but hustling? I was great at it. I just hadn't matched it with the right opportunity yet. Maybe I still had learning to do before the blessings could come.

After Vegas, and with no cops showing up, I felt relief. I went back to my routine. But something was off. I felt hungry again. I wanted more. I needed better connects. My grind felt too small.

My relationship was on and off. The girl I went to Vegas with wasn't the same one from when I got shot. I was older now — not a teenager. I kind of wanted a relationship. I can't explain what the connection was, but this new girl would eventually become the mother of my kids.

The hustle was there, but the opportunity wasn't. I had a lightweight crack hustle going, but my bread and butter was weed — and I was out. Worse, my connect was lagging.

So I started looking. There was this dude I met at the apartments — we had mutual acquaintances. We had talked before. Long shot, but I decided to visit. He stayed on the east side. I drove out there. Ended up being a dry run. Nothing came of it.

On the way back to my apartment, I was bumpin music. I got flagged down by someone I knew. I thought he was just saying what's up. Maybe even pay me some money he owed me. I turn the music down and say, "What up?" He goes, "They raiding your spot right now!"

I said, "What?" He told me to pull up a little bit more.

So I did.

I could see my apartment — swarmed. Police everywhere. I asked if Bam Bam was in there. He said yeah.

Damn.

I knew I had to move. I told him, "I'm out — I gotta get out the way."

I dipped.

Drove past the apartment it felt like slow motion seeing all the police. Went down the block and parked. I had a prepaid burner phone, so I called the apartment landline.

A cop answered.

"Can I speak to Joe?"

"He's busy right now. Who is this?"

Click.

I hung up and got the hell out of there.

Chapter 12

Pressure Building

pressure (noun) 1. Continuous force pushing against something or someone. 2. The tension between survival and collapse.

They were looking for me, but I wasn't looking to be found.

Of course I ran straight to my mom — let her know what had happened. Figured they had to be looking for me. I wasn't exactly sure why they raided the apartment at this point.

Thankfully, I had my re-up money on me and one of my straps. I was out of weed, but I had some chopped-up crack and an SKS assault rifle in my room. The apartment was under both mine and Bam Bam's names.

I couldn't stay at my mom's — that'd be the first place they'd go.

I had a cool relationship with my ex-girl's mom at the time, and she lived in the hood. My ex didn't live there. The hood could be dangerous. I had to stay sharp, all ten toes down. Couldn't get caught slipping. We still had that ongoing inner feud within the gang, and I'm sure they weren't happy with me.

They took Bam Bam in, but he got released. The gun he had was legal. They only found a plate with crack residue near him. But everything else? That was in my room.

2.7 grams of chopped crack. An SKS assault rifle. A bulletproof vest. And $615 stashed in the closet — the exact rent money, with one extra dollar to cover the money order fee.

Chapter 13

<u>Nowhere Feels Safe</u>

paranoia (noun) 1. A state of fear so deep it becomes preparation. 2. When looking over your shoulder feels safer than looking ahead.

I wasn't living anymore. I was calculating. Surviving.

The next day after the raid, I sent my mom to my apartment to get all my stuff. She had my little cousin with her, so I told her I'd watch him and she could take my car — it was under her name anyway. I figured they might be watching. If they saw my car but it wasn't me, I'd know how serious it was.

While she was there, they popped up on her asking about me. She called me, and I grabbed my two-year-old cousin and got out of there. That would be the next place they came. I still didn't know why they raided us. I hadn't spoken to Bam Bam yet.

Turns out Bam sold some crack to an informant. Somebody he didn't trust, but still did the deal. Must've been while I wasn't there. He didn't like the vibe, so he grabbed my assault rifle to make a statement. That same informant told the cops there were guns and drugs in our spot. They got a warrant. They hit our apartment — and another one on the corner — at the same time.

I was just trying to figure out my next move.

Barely a week after the raid, I was at a major intersection using a payphone with some homies. This car kept rolling by, looking off. Didn't recognize them. I brushed it off. We hopped in the homie's car and headed south. Took a right at the next big street — and what do you know, that same car pulls up on us like they wanted something.

I told the homie, "If you pull up next to them, I'm lighting them up."

He did.

And I did.

I wasn't taking chances. I had learned — shoot first.

We hit the corner. I told the homies, "Let me out. I ain't getting caught in the car if the ghetto bird comes." I took my chances on foot. Ran to a small parking lot that led to an alley. That same car doubled back. As I was running, I hit a black-painted chain between two poles. Didn't see it. Bit the dust hard.

Shoe flew off. I heard bullets fly by.

Still had my gun in hand. Jumped up. Fired off a shot. Grabbed my shoe. Took off into the alley. I dipped through back paths and ended up at a homie's house. Borrowed a flannel, grabbed a bike. It was late October, a little cold. Ended the night at my ex-girl's mom's place. Close call.

Next day — Halloween.

We were on alert. Thought the other side might try something. I don't remember all the details, but we were five deep in an SUV with the back window up. We pulled back into the hood and spotted that same little blue Dodge from before. They came off the block behind us.

I know they recognized our SUV.

They weren't expecting what came next.

We started bustin. The homie popped out the passenger window. I was firing out the back. Trick-or-treaters scattered. Another homie yelled, "Bust, bust!" Then Lil Chino said, "I can't," when his clip was empty. I kept pacing it with an extended clip until we hit the corner.

We pulled into the alley.

And I was gone — again.

I'm not speaking on this to brag. I'm explaining how my life was. Where my mind was at. What I'd been through. The ignorant acts I committed. The violence I was involved in.

I'm thankful — once again — that I missed.

And even more thankful none of those trick-or-treaters got hit.

Chapter 14

<u>No Money in War</u>

burnout (noun) 1. Exhaustion caused by prolonged stress or struggle. 2. When even the hustle stops feeling like progress.

There were no shootouts. No glory. Just quiet breakdowns.

The energy was off. There's no money in war.

I wasn't rebuilding anything — just more destruction, every day. So I chilled out. I actually ended up back with my ex-girl. Just stayed low key. Made some money, but nothing major.

November came — my birthday month. Had a little BBQ at my girl's mom's house. Bought myself a T-bone steak and had her mom grill it. First T-bone I ever had in my life.

December hit harder. I was doing worse.

Come Christmas, I had to pawn my video game system just to get some money. I didn't even play it anymore, but it still stung. I was just trying to keep up, stay afloat.

Then came Y2K. The scare was real — stores were out of water, people were panicking. January 1st, 2000 hit.

Nothing changed.

Me and my girl were doing good. No run-ins with the other side. But I was feeling broke. Lost. Flatlined.

My homeboy Chico — Bam Bam's brother — had gone back to prison and just got out. I hadn't seen him since he bolted out the front door back when I got jammed up on that armed robbery.

So of course, we got back to our old ways.

Chapter 15

Jesse James and Billy the Kid

duo (noun) 1. A pair who move in sync. 2. Two people who bring out something in each other that no one else does.

Me and Chico were like Jesse James and Billy the Kid.

There's a lot I could speak on — but there's a lot I can't.

I don't know what it was, but me and Chico just clicked. When we linked up, it was like Jesse James and Billy the Kid.

When I was 14, I was robbing people at random. Got caught. That was risky. At 16, I figured it out — rob trap houses. They can't report it. But yeah... you can still get locked up for that too. So I learned I had to be cautious, even when robbing drug dealers.

With funds low and responsibilities to take care of, me and Chico hit the east side. I was nervous. Last time I robbed a crack house, I got locked up for it.

We found someone. Had him take me to buy some crack. That's how I always got in — acted like a customer. Even dressed the part. Non-matching clothes. Low key. I told the guy I was looking for a 16th.

He took me to the spot. Looked easy.

But as soon as we walked in — boom — they shut and locked the door.

Two guys popped out from behind the couch. One had a revolver. They were speaking Spanish. I barely understood, but I caught the vibe. They thought I was a cop. Told the dude that brought me to make me smoke some of the crack to prove I wasn't.

I told them I smoked it with weed. Back then, they called it primos. Truth is — I'd never smoked crack or a primo in my life. Wasn't about to start then.

They handed me some brown dirt weed. Told me to roll up. I was ready to shoot my way out if I had to. I didn't know what that stuff would do to me, and I wasn't about to get caught slipping. My odds were way lower if I was high.

So I stood on it. Said, "I'm not feelin this. Y'all making me nervous. I'm not smoking that dirt weed. I got forty bucks on a 16th — either you're selling or not."

So yeah — I went to rob someone. And I ended up buying a 16th.

That was the only hiccup. I wasn't about to let that happen again.

After that, we went on a spree.

It got to a point where if they were selling crack on the east side — they were selling it out the window, or with a gun pointed at you the whole time.

It seemed like we were running out of people to rob.

Chapter 16

<u>The Big One</u>

escalation (noun) 1. A rapid increase in intensity or danger. 2. The moment when you stop robbing for survival and start hunting for status.

This wasn't about surviving anymore. This was about the score.

Like I said, me and my girl were on again, off again — and of course, we ended up off AGAIN.

So I was out. Had money stacked up. Hit up the manager at the same apartments I got raided at. Told them the situation was cleared up. They gave me a 1-bedroom upstairs.

This time, it was all me.

I went out, bought all new furniture. Cheap stuff, but I made it look nice — black futon couch, glass dining room table, bedframe, mattress — everything I needed.

Then Chico hits me up. His sister was with this paisa dude who worked for a big dealer. And the goal was different now — we weren't trying to hit little crack spots anymore. We wanted the bricks. Not the ounces.

This was about making a move.

The paisa dude was working out of a spot on the east side — of course. You don't shit in your own backyard.

We set it up. Had his guy bring us an 8-ball — start small. They never roll solo. So he pulls up with a partner. We bring them in. Put them at gunpoint.

Chico talks to them in Spanish. We take everything they got. Search the car. Make his partner strip down naked and lay in the room off to the side. Then we make the one guy call his plug — tell him to pull up with more work.

So now that guy comes. And repeat.

Put them at gunpoint. Make them all strip down. Lay in the room. Search the car. Strip the next one. Same thing.

Cars started stacking up out front. I had to start moving them down the alley.

We kept going. Got all the way up to the big guy's brother. The main dude? Just happened to be in Mexico.

We left all of them naked on the floor. Loaded up everything. Took off.

Went back to my apartment. Divided everything up.

Came up on about a half kilo in coke and rocked-up crack. Jewelry. Cash. Cell phones.

Probably the biggest lick I'd hit at that time.

Chapter 17

<u>High Horse, Low Ground</u>

illusion (noun) 1. A false idea or belief, often dressed up as success. 2. The moment you feel most untouchable but youre actually closest to the edge.

I had it all back. But I still couldn't sleep right.

I was sitting on my high horse at this time — pumped up.

Everything I lost, I got it all right back. And then some.

I still had Detective Jeff Brown wanting to question me about the raid, so that was hanging over my head. I had been stopped and detained a couple times, but they always let me go. No warrant — just detain and try to reach the detective. But he never showed up.

One time, my brother was hiding in my mom's house. The cops had it surrounded. I went to see how I could help and they detained me — really just held me hostage. They even left messages on the answering machine, telling my brother they had me and would let me go if he came out.

He was smart and didn't.

They tried though. Eventually they left. They couldn't prove he was in the house.

Outside of that? Got back with my girl for a minute — but of course, that didn't last long.

So, with my brother hiding from the cops, I bought a couple Greyhound tickets. Stashed some work in my socks.

And we were on our way to Las Vegas.

Chapter 18

<u>Almost Caught Slippin</u>

instinct (noun) A natural ability to act quickly, especially in danger. The only thing between you and a felony charge.

Sometimes the smartest move is the one you make without thinking.

Las Vegas was like a gold mine to me. They liked to go fast and were paying top dollar for the crystal meth I could get dirt cheap. My brother stayed for a little bit with a childhood friend who lived out there, but he didn't last long — he went back home. I stayed with my cousins.

I was bouncing between my female stripper cousin's apartment and her brother's place. I moved all the work I brought and needed to re-up. I wasn't about to catch that Greyhound back — it was a 13-hour ride. Driving took less than half that. I had never been on a plane before, but I was ready to risk it. This was pre-9/11. You could just walk into the airport and pay for the next flight. And I did — $99 for the next flight to Phoenix. I think it was Southwest. So that became the move — get a ride or bus to Vegas, fly back.

I was home, out all night with some homies until the sun came up. We were dropping a homie off at his apartment. I can't recall why, but for some reason, these fools wanted to spray paint the side of a liquor store. I was about to go back to Vegas. I had just re-upped. Six ounces of meth in a black bag. My SUV window didn't work right. The homie lived in a sketchy neighborhood. I wasn't leaving that bag in the car.

I had no business walking over there with them — but I did.

As I'm walking up, a cop pulls up and jumps out. Gun drawn. He puts us all at gunpoint. I turn the other way and try to keep walking like I'm not with them. He yells, "Stop or I'll shoot."

I didn't know what to do. Run? Toss the bag over the fence? I thought fast. Turned around. Walked where he told us. Threw the bag on the ground. Put my hands on the wall.

He patted us down. Told us to sit down. So I sat. Right on the bag.

Either he didn't notice, didn't care, or just forgot about that bag. But after he ran our names, and nothing came back he let us go.

Walked away from that one. Barely.

Chapter 19

<u>From Hustle to Harmony</u>

transition (noun) 1. A process of changing from one state to another. 2. The quiet moment where something bigger than money starts calling.

I wasn't just stacking. I was building.

Like I said, Las Vegas became my home away from home. I loved it out there — and I was making good profit.

I was making trades, flipping things left and right. Ended up with dirt bikes, go-karts, even an ATC. Hustling hard. Moving smart. Making it work.

I even got a car out there that just needed some work.

But on top of all that — my cousin was into music.

Most people didn't know it, but I had been recording little verses for a while. Nothing crazy. Just me with a boombox recorder, playing an instrumental off a bigger stereo and rapping over it. A few friends knew. Nobody else.

But my cousin? He had real equipment. A full setup.

Through the hustle out there, I got my first drum machine and my first sampler.

It wasn't just about money anymore.

I was still in the streets — but something else was starting to pull me. I wasn't just stacking.

I was building.

Chapter 20

<u>Let It Go</u>

restraint (noun) 1. The ability to hold back when you're fully capable of reacting. 2. A silent form of strength that doesnt need applause.

The old me would've fired. The new me walked away.

While I was out in Las Vegas, I called the homies to check in — see how things were in the hood. Got bad news.

My homeboy Lil Chino had been killed.

Right there in the hood.

We suspected the other side caught him slipping. They found him with his gun still in hand and a beer sat perfectly on the sidewalk beside him. Word was, he had just left the plug — walking home after he went to re-up.

Years later, someone from the other side claimed the fame. But we never really found out what happened.

I came back to Phoenix. Let go of my apartment. I was spending more time in Vegas anyway. Took what I needed to my mom's. Told my ex-girl's mom she could have the furniture if anyone needed it.

I went to the hood to go see how everything was. Ended up taking Lil Chino's brother to collect some money from a homie that owed him.

We pull up.

And I get into a slight argument over some old beef. The fools mom and uncle come outside. His uncle starts acting tough. He gives me a little one-handed push.

I reach for my Glock.

I say, "Push me one more time."

This was a grown man. I had been through a lot. But I was still just a 19-year-old kid.

And he pushed me again.

I just gritted my teeth and let it go.

Too many witnesses. People already talking about calling the cops. So we left.

Sometimes walking away is harder than pulling the trigger.

Chapter 21

Charged It to the Game

evolution (noun) 1. The process of growth through pain, pressure, and restraint. 2. When you stop proving you're dangerous, and start proving you're disciplined.

I had the .357. I had the reason. I chose something else.

I ended up selling my Glock to get more crystal to take to Las Vegas, along with my re-up. Figured I could come back and buy an even better gun with the extra money I'd make.

Tying up all my loose ends before I left the state again. I couldn't run around without protection, so I came up on a .357.

It had been about a week since that altercation — where that fools uncle pushed me.

It was nighttime, kind of late. I stopped by the house in the hood where we all used to kick it — Lil Chino's brother's spot. There was a homegirl on the porch that I had never met.

And wouldn't you know it — there he was. That fools uncle that pushed me.

He didn't say anything as I walked up. I sat down. Chilled. Quiet.

He was talking to the homegirl. I'm sitting there planning it in my head. He's gonna leave. Walk through the alley. And I got this .357.

No shell casings. Clean.

Still sitting there, quiet. Waiting.

Then he looks at me and says, "I seen you here before, haven't I?"

I lost my composure. I stood up and said, "You know who the f**k I am. Don't play with me."

Made a scene. And just like that — if anything happened to him after that — it'd point right back to me.

Now that I think about it... would it really have been worth it?

Take this man's life and risk doing life — for what?

For a grown man trying to act tough to a kid?

Yeah, he's a piece of shit. No doubt. But his karma will come to him. As a matter of fact it did I dropped that fool two times outside of a bar later on in life after he disrespected me, better that then me killing him.

But I ended up losing that .357 anyway. I was at a hotel room before I left back to Vegas. Don't recall what happened exactly, security came knocking with the cops to kick everyone out.

Instead of getting searched and catching a charge — I slipped the gun behind the mini fridge.

Charged it to the game.

Chapter 22

<u>They Came for Me</u>

consequence (noun) 1. A result or effect of a past decision. 2. The part of the game nobody raps about.

You play long enough, they come knocking.

Vegas was good — but it was slowing down this time.

The money wasn't coming as fast. People I was dealing with started getting better product than the cheap stuff I was taxing them on. Still made decent profit, but I could feel the change.

I came back to Phoenix. Left Vegas with people owing me money. Left the car I never fixed up. Took my music gear back home and started adding to it — making beats, recording myself.

But first thing I had to do when I got back?

Get a new strap.

After Lil Chino got killed, no way I was gonna roll through the hood without one.

Heard one of the homeboys got into his dad's safe full of military-style guns. Dude was known for talking about that safe. Now he had it open.

Pulled up. Worked a deal. Grabbed a MAC-10 with a silencer and an AR-15.

Was hard to get him to come off those. But a week later he started letting them go more freely to other homies. So I doubled back and grabbed what was left.

I was staying at my mom's again — planning to head back to Vegas.

Then one morning, I was sleeping on the couch.

My mom woke me up. Said some guy from a temp agency called looking for me. She already knew something was off — "You ain't looking for no job." I wasn't.

We knew it was the police.

I called the number back from my burner. The guy had an attitude. I said I got a page with the code 27. He said no one paged me. I asked if it was a business or a home phone. He said business but its his personal line.

I just hung up.

Didn't know what it had to do with — but I knew it was the cops.

Stashed the guns in the closet. Took a shower. I ain't trying to get locked up feeling dirty.

We noticed a truck across the street just sitting there.

My mom had to go pick up my sister. I told her, "Take my SUV — see what happens."

She pulls off. Nothing.

Then a different truck pulls into the cul-de-sac. Bumps my stepdad's truck. Guy gets out and walks toward the house. My stepdad cracks the door. Dude starts asking if we want to sell the car in the driveway.

My stepdad says the guy who owns it ain't here. Shooed him away.

Then my mom pulls back up. He stops her. Starts talking about the car.

My little sister comes in. I tell her, "What's mom doing? That's a cop."

Told her keep eyes on the other truck across the street.

I throw on my shoes. Come back ask about the truck. She says no movement. I say, "Okay, thanks."

Now I figure — if they're here for me, and I go outside, they don't need to come in. So I step out.

He sees me. Eyes get big. Tries to keep up the act. Starts asking me about the car.

I say, "I don't know nothin about it."

He asks if I know how to open the trunk — in that car that is where the motor is.

I say nope.

But that must've been the signal.

As soon as he popped that trunk — unmarked SUVs and trucks flood the cul-de-sac.

Guns drawn.

It was a mixed task force.

They ask who I am. I say, "You know who I am. You're here for me."

I ask, "Where's Detective Jeff Brown?"

He says, "Who's that?"

Chapter 23

<u>Not Even Shook</u>

threshold (noun) 1. The point where something begins to shift. 2. The place between freedom and time served.

They didn't break me. They barely surprised me.

I asked about Detective Jeff Brown just to get a feel for what this was. I didn't know if it was about something new or if it went back to my apartment getting raided a year earlier.

But when they didn't even know who Jeff Brown was — that's when I got nervous.

This wasn't just local. These were FBI agents. This was a full sting operation just for me.

They patted me down and put me in the passenger seat of an unmarked truck. One of the agents — the one in the driver's seat — told me he was part of an FBI task force.

I said, "Damn, FBI? Y'all treating me like I'm John Gotti or something."

Another agent came up to the window, told him something. Then the agent turned to me and said, "Detective Brown doesn't want to talk to you. Said you told him to go f*** off."

At that moment — I knew it wasn't that bad.

They didn't go inside. Didn't search the house. They came for me. And they got me.

I could deal with that.

They booked me in. My bond was $3,500. That's light. I'd never gotten it that easy before. So I wasn't even stressed. I had $3,200 at home. I figured I'd be out before I even hit a bunk.

They classified me minimum custody. Sent me to Durango Jail. It was overcrowded. I had a mat on the floor in the day room. But I didn't plan on being there long.

Still, for some reason — it took my mom about a week to get me out.

But this was new for me. I had never been released pending court before. They always hit me with high bonds or kept me detained. Now I was out.

And the charges? They felt weak.

This time, I was gonna fight from the outside.

Chapter 24

<u>My Name Came Up</u>

accusation (noun) 1. A claim or charge of wrongdoing, true or not. 2. A street death sentence when said to the wrong people.

I wasn't gonna wait around to prove I was innocent. I moved.

After that scare, my stepdad packed up all the guns and took them to his mom's house for safekeeping. I had a 9mm to run around with, so I was good. Let the rest stay stashed for now — especially while I was out on bond.

Funds were low after paying the bond. Had to get back on the grind.

Vegas was off the table for a while. I wasn't trying to blow my bond terms.

At this point, I was all over the place. Crack was the main bread and butter, but I had weed, some liquid acid, some glass, and even got into cooking meth.

Started having people steal Sudafed pill packs from stores, pulling the ephedrine out and trying to cook small batches. Found a feed store in Black Canyon City that sold iodine. Had a few connects come through with red phosphorus. But that was all trial and error.

I had a guy who knew the process, but something always went wrong. The batches didn't come out perfect. It took too much time. And the charge for manufacturing was steep.

I had to get my priorities straight. All that experimenting with other drugs was throwing off my crack re-up. In the end, I was making less money than if I just stuck to one product.

Crack.

I had been hanging around the hood, kicking it at Lil Chino's brother's house. Started hanging more with Lil Chino's cousin too.

Then one evening — I get a call.

Lil Chino's brother got murdered. In that same house. In his room. Hit in the head with a sledgehammer or something. I never got to see the report.

One of his cousins was even sleeping on the couch when it happened.

I had to make my way to the hood to see what's up. But something felt off. Energy was wrong.

Down the block at Lil Chino's baby momma's house, a few homies were posted. Lil Chino's cousin was there too. I'm talking to him — and he hits me with it:

"Just so you know, your name came up. Something about if he got shot with .45, you got one with a silencer..."

I said, "Oh yeah? Is that right?"

Now I'm not feeling it at all.

It was like someone was trying to set me up. Put the blame on me for something I didn't do.

Even in a conversation another time, a homegirl told me that Lil Chino's brother's son told her, "Lazy Wedo killed my dad." When she went over there.

But after he said that.

I looked at Lil Chino's cousin and said, "Check this out — since you saying this, I gotta go to my house and take care of some things. I'ma be back."

I rushed to the house. Went straight to my room.

Grabbed all my ephedrine. All my cooking supplies. All my other drugs. Had to find a place to stash everything, just in case.

Chapter 25

They Wanted Me to Be Him

misidentification (noun) 1. Being confused for someone else but suffering the consequences anyway. 2. A warning that your name is louder than you think.

They hit his apartment hoping he was me. That's when I knew they're closing in.

I got focused. Got rid of everything. Watched who I was around. And stuck to the bread and butter.

About a month before Lil Chino's brother got murdered, the homie who got into his dad's safe and sold me the guns got caught up on a violation. Headed to state prison. I made sure I sent word to the other homies inside to look out for him.

I had a longtime homie from the hood doing a flat 11 for a murder in state prison. We kept in touch.

When the cops went to Lil Chino's brother's house to investigate the murder, I don't know everything they found. But I do know they recovered a rifle that was linked to those same guns from that safe.

So it wasn't long before Lil Chino's cousin — who also lived there — got locked up too.

The hood was hot.

But I was focused.

Only selling crack. Messing around with some music. Trying to record a few songs. I was meeting more people into rapping. Even my homie doing time was into it. If I could make something happen before he got out in 2008, that'd be dope.

I wasn't chasing a rap career. I was thinking bigger.

I wanted to be Eazy-E. Or Master P, something like Suge Knight. The business guy. Use the dope money to fund something real. Build a legitimate product. No more watching my back every second. No more running from the cops. Just live.

I used to watch MTV Cribs and feel it in my gut — That's gonna be me one day.

I was gonna have it like that.

There was a homie from the hood named Huero. He had already been to prison. He was on gang file and all that.

The cops were looking for someone named Lazy Huero — someone those guns were traced back to.

I'd been nicknamed Wedo since I was a preteen. Spelled it different. They started calling me Lazy Wedo cause I'd sleep my time off in jail. I would also sleep all day after selling crack all night. That name just stuck. Separated me from all the other homies named Huero in the hood.

But they hit Huero's apartment — thinking he was me.

They locked up Lil Chino's cousin. They raided Huero's spot.

And I already knew — They were closing in.

Chapter 26

<u>No Going Back</u>

premeditation (noun) 1. The act of planning something before it happens especially violence. 2. The clearest sign you've lost the line between survival and destruction.

At that point, I wasn't reacting. I was deciding.

It was winter — but it was hot out.

And I'm not talking about the weather.

That didn't hold me back one bit.

My crime partner Chico — he was the one with the plug on the crack through the paisas. I was re-upping with an eighth of a key every time. I didn't want to get ahead of myself.

One day I go to re-up, and he hits me up.

He says there's a lick if I want it.

He tells me about these paisas — two guys and their tia, an older lady — living in some townhomes close to the hood. He says they're about to head to Mexico. He says they've got at least $100K in cash, probably still got some work too.

He tells me, "You got those toys. Be perfect for that job."

I said, "Hell yeah. Let me go get them. Let's do this."

I had my stepdad grab the silencers and guns from his mom's house where they'd been stashed. He gets them. I'm on my way back to Chico's.

Chico calls up the inside guy — the one giving him the info. That guy's coming with me. He brings along another paisa too.

Chico isn't going — but I make sure to take his nephew. Me and him are tight. He's like family. I know I can trust him.

And to be honest?

After we hit this lick...

Only me and nephew are leaving.

That was the plan.

These other two? Nah.

I got a silencer. All you're gonna hear is metal hitting metal. I'm knocking on that door — and when they answer? Everyone there is getting one to the head. Take what they got. Then take out the other two who came with us. No witnesses. No splits.

Just me and my guy.

That's the plan.

No going back.

Chapter 27

<u>The Line I Didn't Cross</u>

conscience (noun) The quiet voice that speaks loudest when you're alone. The reason some people survive and others lose their soul.

I could've done it. But I would've never been the same.

We pulled up to the townhouses. I had black latex gloves on. I was ready. The guy pointed out which one it was.

I got out the car and walked around to see what I could see. Nothing. No movement. No signs. I got back in the car and started questioning the guy.

"How do you know they got money in there? Did you see it?"

I started second-guessing the whole thing. What if this guy gave me bad information? What if...

They had no clue what my plan really was and what I was ready to do.

And then I started thinking—there's a lady in there.

I couldn't leave any witnesses. But I couldn't hurt this lady either.

It is what it is. It's a no-go.

When I got home, I stashed the MAC-10 and the silencers under the bathroom sink. My bathroom connected to my mom and stepdad's room, but it was blocked off on their side. Like my own private bathroom. I pulled out the baseboard—nobody would ever know it moved. Slid everything in there.

Didn't give them back to my stepdad. Even though I knew the cops would probably come sooner or later, I didn't panic. I let him know. Told him they were stashed good and where. That way I also had easy access to them if needed.

Meanwhile, I was still out on bond fighting the case from the raid. They charged me with misconduct involving weapons and narcotics for sale. They were trying to give me probation and six months county time.

I said I'd take probation—but no county time. I ain't doing that.

Eventually, they agreed. They dropped the weapons charge. Dropped the other charge down to simple possession of narcotics. Put me on a Prop 200 drug court program. Got that out the way.

I didn't mind probation. Most people hate it because they can't stay clean. That's not an issue for me.

I don't use.

Chapter 28

The Plan That Didn't Stick

conflict (noun) A battle between two opposite forces. Wanting change while still doing the same thing.

I had a plan. But the streets had one too.

Part of the terms of probation was I had to go to school or work. Well, I wasn't trying to work a 9 to 5. I was doing well with what I was doing. I had tried to work regular jobs a few times—it just wasn't my thing.

Like I said before, I was smart. I could learn fast. I honestly believe I could've run a company. I liked business. That's probably why I was good at selling dope.

I had a meeting with the people at A.I.B.T.—Arizona Institute of Business and Technology. They were trying to sell me on student loans and get me into business classes. But first, I had to get my GED. They had free classes for that there.

So that was the plan. GED classes at AIBT. Keep the PO happy. Keep hustling.

That plan didn't come together though.

I had a long day hustling. Picked up a re-up—eighth of a key, already rocked up. Opened it up. Broke off a couple pieces from one of the big cookies of crack. Sold my last 16th for the night.

Hit up Filiberto's—the Mexican spot right by my mom's house. Grabbed a late-night plate for me and my little sister.

Went home. Ate. Went an put on a movie in my room. Chilled out. And got some sleep.

Chapter 29

<u>It Finally Caught Up</u>

inevitable (adjective) 1. Certain to happen; unavoidable. 2. What you see coming but still aren't ready for.

They didn't surprise me. But they still got me.

Next thing I knew, I woke up to the front door being crashed in and hearing, ATF! We have a warrant!

I jumped up quick. Grabbed my 9mm and stashed it under the bathroom sink with the MAC-10 and silencers. Shoved my re-up deep into my Nike Cortez shoes by the bed.

Still in my boxers and a muscle shirt. I grabbed some shorts, a shirt, and a different pair of shoes. Opened my bedroom door.

As soon as I stepped into the hallway—SWAT stepped around the corner. Shields. Helmets. Assault rifles.

Drop it!

I said, It's my clothes.

Drop it!

So I did.

They grabbed me. Rushed me out the house. It was late February, around 6-something in the morning. Cold. I'm standing out there in my underwear.

They had my mom, my sister, and my stepdad outside too.

They asked me if I was willing to talk. I said yeah. I wasn't gonna admit anything—but I figured it was the best way to learn what they knew. Feed them lies or half-truths. Buy time.

But truth is?

The best move was to lawyer up.

They asked if I knew the homie I got the guns from—and Lil Chino's cousin—by their government names. Asked if I knew anything about stolen guns.

I said yeah, I know who those individuals are—that much was obvious.

But I don't know nothing about no guns.

I already had a feeling what this was about.

But now?

I knew exactly what was going on.

Chapter 30

<u>I Knew What This Was</u>

acceptance (noun) 1. The moment you stop fighting what you know is already true. 2. When the front you put up finally cracks into truth.

They didn't even have to push me. I walked into it.

They took my whole family and had us sit on the couch while they continued searching. I expected to be cuffed up already—but they let me put on the shirt and shorts I had in my hands earlier.

My mom was having a low blood sugar episode, probably from all the stress. They allowed me to make her some toast.

Then they took me into my room. Two agents questioned me some more. They asked if the bedroom and attached bathroom were mine.

I said, yes. This bedroom and bathroom are mine. Nobody else in the house uses them. Everything in there is mine.

The agents nodded. One pointed to some valuables—gold chains, a Movado watch, some cash. I said, Yeah, that's all mine.

There was a door in my room that led to the outside—right next to my bed. They had me stand against it and took pictures of my tattoos.

I looked down and saw my Nike Cortez shoes. One was kicked over.

And that's when I saw it.

A couple loose rocks—just lying there on the carpet, kind of blending in. But I saw them. And I was stressing.

I had a '78 Monte Carlo I had just taken off Chico's hands. They asked if they could search it. Knowing there was nothing in there—and hoping it would distract them—I said, Go ahead.

About 30 minutes later, another agent asked if I was still willing to answer questions.

I stayed cool. Nonchalant. Said, yeah, sure.

He said, we found narcotics, U.S. currency, a machine gun, handgun, and silencers in your bedroom and attached bathroom.

I got a little nervous. I think it showed.

They asked me if those items belonged to me.

I said, the cash is mine.

They asked again—about the machine gun, the silencers, the weapons.

I said, I don't know anything.

Then they asked, Why did you have a machine gun, handgun, and silencers in your bathroom?

I was agitated. Caught.

I said, if someone gave you something for free, you'd take it, right?

Then I added, I ain't sayin' nothing. But that is my room and that is my bathroom.

Chapter 31

<u>Nowhere to Run</u>

federal (adjective) 1. Belonging to a system bigger than your neighborhood, your city, or your state. 2. The part of the game that feels like you're up against a whole country.

They weren't playing with me. And I couldn't talk my way out.

By about 10am, ATF took me into custody and walked me out the front door. My mom was outside.

She asked, Where are you taking him?

The agent said, Oh, he's looking at 30 years.

I yelled out, I love you, Mom! Don't listen to him!

That pissed me off. He was trying to stress her out. As he put me in the ATF vehicle, I told him, You lucky my mom was home or I woulda came out busting.

He asked, What do you mean?

I said, If my mom wasn't there, I woulda came out shooting.

They took me to the U.S. Marshals office in downtown Phoenix. Processed me in their system. Fingerprinted me. Gave me a federal number: 45906-008.

They asked if I wanted to drop a UA for pretrial services. I agreed. I was clean—I don't do drugs—so I figured that would help.

After a while, I had my initial detention hearing. They informed me of my rights, the charges, all that. And they kept me detained. No bond.

Stuck like Chuck.

This was all new to me. I'd been to juvenile. County jail on the minors floor. Even county as an adult. But this?

This was federal.

When I went to court, it wasn't the State of Arizona vs. me

It was the United States of America vs. me.

Like I made enemies with the whole country.

The charges:
Count 1 – Felon in possession of a firearm
Count 2 – Possession of a silencer
Count 3 – Possession of a machine gun
Count 4 – Possession with intent to distribute a controlled substance (cocaine)
Count 5 – Using a firearm during a drug trafficking crime

It wasn't looking good.

But the crazy part? They never even found the crack—right under their nose.

They did find about 2 ounces of powder coke I had in a pair of Converse All Stars under my raised-up dresser. And when they gave me some shoes to wear?

Those were the ones they gave me.

They put me in a holding tank—just people coming in and out of court. Mostly all paisas. One said something in Spanish. Another guy translated.

He said good thing you like those shoes. Where we goin, they gonna give you a pair just like that.

I just laughed. Beats the pink socks and boxers with black-and-white stripes in county jail.

Eventually they shackled up our legs, chained our waists, and hit us with the black box cuffs. Put us on a bus from Phoenix to CCA—Corrections Corporation of America. A private prison in Florence, Arizona.

They had a contract with the U.S. Marshals to house federal inmates.

And that's where they sent me.

Chapter 32

<u>Like a Whole Different Country</u>

displacement (noun) 1. The feeling of being in the right body but the wrong place. 2. When nobody around you knows who you really are but someone outside is rewriting your name.

I didn't know where I belonged. But I knew I didn't belong there.

We get to CCA and they get us off the bus. As I'm walking in, I hear someone yell out, Wedgewood! That's my gang—Wedgewood Chicanos, 48th Avenue.

It caught me off guard. Turned out it was the gang investigator for the prison.

He says, Your homeboy is here in the 1200 unit. Want me to put you over there with him?

I'm like, nah I'm good.

He was talking about Lil Chino's cousin. He had already been locked up. And I knew—deep down—the only way they came for me was somebody had to snitch. I just didn't know who.

They throw me in a smelly holding tank packed with paisas. I'm stuck in there for a while. Long day.

I'm tired. I'm worried about my family. I feel like I'm locked up in a whole different country.

Eventually they dress me out in green jail scrubs and some black canvas Bob Barker shoes. The kind that looked just like my Converse. That paisa wasn't lying.

They take us in a group to an orientation unit. I get thrown in an 8-man cell.

I just laid on my bunk. Depression started creeping in. Mind racing. Couldn't sleep. No familiar faces to talk to.

That's one thing I liked about county jail—you always ran into someone you knew or who knew somebody.

For the next day or so I kept to myself. Then a couple days in, I was eating lunch and a homeboy walked up with another guy.

He tells the guy, Let's sit here with homeboy.

He starts talking to me. Turns out he's from Tempe—from a neighborhood called La Victoria. Even crazier? He lives on the west side, next door to one of my homies named Spooky.

It was good to have someone to chop it up with. I started to feel like I was easing in.

I mean—I had to. I wasn't going anywhere.

One day homie from La Victoria is on the phone. He calls me over and hands me the phone.

It's Spooky.

He's like, What's up homie? What you doing there?

Then out of nowhere, he says, Ay, I heard you killed Lil Chino's brother.

I said, Whoa. Who said that? I'm like nah. But don't say that on this phone.

I handed the phone back.

That blew my mind. Who knows what people were saying out there. That's all I needed—for them to try to throw that on me too.

I know I didn't do it.

But I had enough to deal with already.

About a week in, they moved us out of orientation into general population. Me and the homie from La Victoria both got sent to the 1200 unit—but into different pods.

I got housed in 1200-A. He went to 1200-B.

All of us going to A pod walked in and everyone's staring—trying to figure out who just came in, what group or race we're with.

I'm white—but I'm from a Chicano gang.

In juvenile, I was just a gang member. But in prison? Race and politics matter.

At this point? I didn't care about any of that.

I just wanted to fight my case.

I just wanted to go home.

CCA was different. Majority paisas—Mexicans from Mexico. Everyone else was outnumbered.

In my pod we had:
4 white guys
3 Sureños
4 Chiefs
1 Black guy well he was Jamaican
And me.

The rest?
All paisas.

Out of 50 to 60 of us—I was just trying to hold my ground.

Chapter 33

<u>Sounded Real Good from Where I Was Sitting</u>

reprieve (noun) 1. A sudden break from a heavy sentence. 2. When the weight doesn't leave but the bars do.

I didn't expect to go home. But I walked out lighter than I came in.

I'm not feeling being at this place. I just want to go home.

But at least I got to make some phone calls. Talked to some people. Some family.

Talked to my mom she was okay, but her and my stepdad were going through it. She was still shaken up.

But like always—she had my back.

I had a court date early on, and I was blessed.

My public defender?

A beast.

There was one ATF agent—straight up, you could tell he couldn't stand me. I'm not even sure what the hearing was about or why he was there. Must've been some motion my public defender put in.

Because that ATF agent had to take the stand.

He gave his little run-down about the firearms. But then my lawyer started pressing:

By looking at that gun—not being trained in firearms and not firing that gun—would you be able to tell that it was a fully automatic machine gun?

The ATF agent said, No.

Do you have any knowledge that my client ever fired that gun?

No.

By looking at that silencer—and not being a trained individual like yourself—would you be able to tell the difference between that silencer and a flash suppressor?

No.

Was there any drugs on the search warrant?

No. Only guns and ammunition.

So you were looking for guns in a pair of shoes?

No, but there could have been bullets there.

Then my public defender dropped it:

Your Honor, I motion to dismiss all charges.

I wasn't quite sure what was going on—but it was sounding real good from where I was sitting.

And the judge...

Dismissed the charges.

Chapter 34

<u>Even in Limbo, I Had to Stand on Something</u>

principle (noun) 1. A code you follow when no one else will. 2. What you protect when you ain't got nothing else to lose.

I didn't know when I was getting out. But I knew I wasn't letting that slide.

I thought I was going home.

But my public defender broke it down—if they released me, they'd pick me right back up as I walked out the door. They were going to re-indict me.

It felt like I was sitting in limbo after that. I was locked up, but I didn't even have a court date for a while.

Eventually I got re-indicted.

New charges:
Count 1 – Felon in possession of a firearm
Count 2 – Possession of unregistered firearms
Count 3 – Possession of unregistered firearms
Count 4 – Possession of unregistered firearms

Looking back, that was a victory.

But I didn't fully comprehend it at the time.

I started getting settled in. Comfortable even.

I got a job in the kitchen making a dollar a day so I could get a little extra commissary. I didn't like asking people for much while I was locked up.

One day, I come back to the pod after work. Go to get my laundry bag out the bin.

My bag was there.

But my laundry wasn't.

We could buy muscle shirts, white tees, and boxers off the canteen. Otherwise, it was standard issue tighty whities. Somebody stole my laundry.

In a place like that? That should be a major violation.

I was a young hothead. I went to the paisa who handled laundry—Flaco.

He said, I just do the laundry and bring it in. Everyone goes through it.

I'm like, Okay.

Then I start yelling out to the whole pod—

Whoever took my laundry is a punk bitch!

One of the shot callers for the paisas—a Border Brother—tries to calm me down.

He says, Ay, calm down bro. Let's figure this out.

I said, Hell nah. You know ain't nobody supposed to be stealing. Somebody better bring me my what they stole!

He calls out to everyone, Who took his stuff?

Nobody speaks up.

Everybody acts like they don't know.

The Border Brother looks at me and says, What you wanna do?

I said, I wanna go to each cell and we look.

He said, Okay. Come on.

We start going cell to cell. Got through like the first five and I gave up.

Lost cause.

I walked right back to the middle of the pod and yelled again—

Whoever took my laundry—you know who you are. And you a bitch!

Chapter 35

<u>Tension in Every Direction</u>

suspicion (noun) 1. A quiet voice in your head that doesn't let you rest. 2. The feeling of being surrounded even when nobody says your name.

I wasn't looking for problems. But they were always within reach.

The cells in my pod were 3-man cells. I had two paisa cellies. They were cool—even tried to teach me a little Spanish. I tried to help them with some English.

Spent most my days working in the kitchen, so I was out of the pod. When I was in the pod, I played cards, listened to my little AM/FM radio, or watched TV.

I never really chose a group or race to run with. I was kind of in my own world. I sat with anybody I could communicate with, the Whites, Chiefs, Sureños, It didn't matter to me.

I finally ran into Lil Chino's cousin in the hall.
He said, "I heard you were here."
Then told me, "When they do church—go. I'll see you there."

His vibe and energy seemed cool. I didn't really trust him, but he was a familiar face from the neighborhood—someone I knew from the outs. That was good to see, even if the trust wasn't there.

I wasn't a religious person. Honestly, I didn't like church. I disliked when people got all preachy or told you everything you were doing was wrong—like you had to follow their way, the church's way, or else. I really didn't like fools that got locked up and all of a sudden find God and hide behind the bible but didn't stick to it.

I gave church a chance. I tried a few times. I just never resonated with it. Maybe I wasn't ready.

They called the service and I went. Lil Chino's cousin was there. We got to chop it up a little bit. He seemed into the church stuff. I was just there to see what he had to say.

There was a time on the outs when we kicked it kind of tough. So maybe I didn't have a reason not to trust him. If he snitched—would he still be there?

He said my name came up when Lil Chino's brother got murdered. But that was his cousin—and he's not showing any resentment toward me.

Maybe I'm tripping.

I didn't make church a habit. Not long after that, Lil Chino's cousin got moved to the 600 unit.

I hadn't seen the homeboy from La Victoria. He had got out, then I heard he came back—and he was in the 600 unit too.

One day I went to work in the kitchen. I wasn't feeling it. I had a headache. I asked the kitchen staff lady if I could go home, back to my pod.

She said, "Yeah. Just get the serving spoons from the dishwashers and bring them to me, then you can go."

I went to the dishwashers. One was a young paisa I didn't know. The other was an older paisa.

I asked for the spoons. I don't think they understood—there was a communication problem. Seemed like the young one caught an attitude.

I had a headache. I wasn't having it.

I got attitude back, I was like, "Just give me the spoons."

They did. I went and gave them to the kitchen staff lady.

Then as I was leaving one of the older paisas came to me.

He said, "What's going on?"

He told me, "That guy is younger and smaller than you."

But really? He wasn't much younger or smaller.

I told him, "I ain't trippin, but it don't matter if it's the biggest guy in here. If you run your mouth to him—you gonna have to deal with it." —and went to my pod.

Chapter 36

Pressure Will Find You

retaliation (noun) 1. The instinct to hit back harder than you were hit. 2. The moment anger becomes its own kind of sentence.

I was cool yesterday. Today, I wasn't having it.

I didn't go to work the next day. I wasn't feeling good. I just chilled in the pod.

The following day, I went to work. I rolled up in the kitchen, not even thinking about that little drama at the dishwashing station. That was a couple days ago. I thought it was done.

First thing, this paisa comes up to me. He's probably a little shorter than me, but older and stockier.

He says, "You said you wanna fight the biggest paisa in here? Well, you can fight me. Let's go."

I said, "I didn't say that. But let's go."

So we walk into a side storage room and square up. Right when I go to take a swing—this short Border Brother comes from the side.

I get jumped.

The Correctional Officers or staff didn't really see what happened, but they knew something happened—I got a black eye.

I told them I slipped and fell.

They took me to the captain's office. The captain asked what happened.

I said, "I slipped and fell. Hit my face on the counter. The floor was wet."

He looked at me and said, "I know you got jumped."

I stuck to my story. "I slipped and fell."

He said, "I'm going to send you back to your pod. If I see you again for any reason—you're going to the hole."

I went back to my pod. I was pissed. Everyone felt the tension. I was planning my move.

That short Border Brother lived in my pod, but I planned to handle it in the kitchen the next day.

Came time to go to work—I was ready. Still heated, I put my hat on and went down to the kitchen.

My intention was to bust someone in the head with a tuna can or something I could cause damage with.

I walked in, and that same paisa was right there, talking about, "What's up?" Like he wanted to fight heads up now.

Heads up was yesterday. Today I'm grabbing a weapon.

I just needed to get close enough to something solid.

We're exchanging words and the paisa's making a scene. The CO steps in before I can get to anything.

They take me to the captain again. This time, he sends me to the hole.

Still angry. I told the CO that took me down to the hole,
"You better not put me with no paisa."

Chapter 37

Locked In, but Wide Awake

*solitude (noun) 1. The kind of quiet that speaks louder than noise ever could.
2. A space where pain, memory, and clarity all sit at the same table.*

I wasn't free. But I was clear.

Going to the hole is like jail inside of jail. They gave us rec for an hour once every three days or so. Just a patio in a small cage—nothing there but air and maybe some sun. I'd be able to appreciate it now, but back then? Nah. I never went.

Any time they took you out of your cell, you were cuffed up. Even just to take a shower, which was also in a cage about 20 feet from my cell. Showers were every other day, if I remember right. I took a lot of bird baths, so it didn't matter to me.

Most of the time in the hole, I was by myself. It was like a getaway. A vacation.

I needed that alone time. I've always been like that. I like to be alone in my own thoughts—to process things, reflect.

I talked to my neighbor here and there. He was a Native named Black Bear. He passed me a couple books to read. They also brought a cart with books every so often.

I've always been into reading. I like literature that gives you knowledge. I like psychology. I didn't mind a good John Grisham book either.

One book I read in the hole was kind of religious. The part that stuck with me was about prayer. About God. It said something like:

What happens when two people are praying for the opposite thing?

A girl prays her relationship works out, and her mother's praying she leaves that man. Whose prayer gets answered?

The book didn't give a clear answer, but that question stuck with me. Later on, it made a lot more sense to me—when it came to energy. What some might call spirituality.

I worked out. Mostly just did push-ups. I wasn't creative with exercise. I never liked burpees. They seemed counterproductive—hard on the joints. Easy way to get hurt, and in there? You don't want to have any disadvantages if it's time for war.

After a few weeks, they brought me a celly—and he was a paisa.

I stood up. The door opens. I'm ready to take off on him.

I look at him—he already had two black eyes. He got jumped in intake.

I wasn't going to take my anger out on him. He wasn't who I wanted to hurt.

Turns out, he was just there for illegally crossing the border. Not in a gang. Didn't know anything about prison politics.

As long as he respected the cell etiquette and wasn't disrespectful—I could deal with him.

He was only there about a week. Then I think they deported him back to Mexico.

Chapter 38

<u>I Had to Pick a Side</u>

alignment (noun) 1. When your actions match your instincts. 2. What happens when neutral ain't safe anymore.

I didn't want to pick a side. But if I didn't, they'd choose one for me.

I had started to go to a counselor early on at CCA, telling them I was having trouble sleeping. She asked questions—I kind of bullshitted her.

I did feel a little depressed. Who wouldn't be? Locked up, away from your loved ones. It's a depressing place.

I really was having issues getting to sleep. I was stressed out, but my brain never really shuts off. It's been that way since I was a kid. So, I played the part to get something to help me sleep.

Honestly, I think they'll prescribe you anything depending on what you say. I saw guys come in normal and end up doing the Thorazine shuffle.

They switched my meds around. Started with Elavil, then Celexa. Even tried to give me Depakote. I didn't like that one. It was like this rubbery, football-shaped thing with liquid inside. I didn't take it long.

The only one that helped me sleep was Elavil.

By the time I got out the hole—I didn't even need it anymore.

They released a few of us from the hole at the same time. Wouldn't you know it—the Border Brother who tried to help me before with the laundry incident, he got out too. We both end up in the pill line.

Guess who else was there?

The paisa from the kitchen. The one I got into it with.

I'm trying to figure out how to play this smart. I'm outnumbered.

We're giving each other dirty looks. Think he said something to that Border Brother.

Me and the Border Brother end up at the pill window at the same time. He says, "Ay man, what's up? These guys wanna get you right now."

I said, "It is what it is."

He tells me, "Be cool. We'll work it out."

I ain't trying to work it out. I want revenge. But I know—I gotta be cool right now. If I react, I'm just getting jumped again. Sent back to the hole.

So I keep my cool. Still giving that paisa dirty looks—but I move on to my new housing unit: 600.

I pass the laundry room. The homie from La Victoria is there. I stop. Talk to him. Tell him a little about what's going on.

He's like, "What are you doing? You know you belong with us." Meaning the Chicanos.

I said, "I know. But I ain't even tripping on all this race and politics stuff. I'm just trying to fight my case and go home."

He told me, "It don't work like that though."

Come to find out, I guess others had already talked about my situation. A white dude—not even from Arizona—a Nazi Lowrider from Cali in 700 unit had put a green light on me for the paisas.

Didn't even talk to me. Didn't even know who I was running with.

The homie from La Victoria told me since I hadn't made it clear who I was running with when I got jumped, there wasn't much they could do. But he said, "You over here with us now, you good."

At this time, tension with the Border Brothers and paisas was already high. A homie named Tommy Guns from 1200 had just gotten into it bad with them. Sent to the hole. Heard it involved locks in socks and some more.

While we're talking, that same Border Brother who tried to help me walks up. Starts talking to the homie from La Victoria.

The homie tells me, "Catch you later."

I let them chop it up and I continue on to my new pod.

Chapter 39

<u>The Picture Got Clearer</u>

*revelation (noun) 1. When the truth shows up and it knows your name.
2. That moment you realize you weren't being paranoid. You were being
followed.*

They were looking for Lazy Huero. And now, they knew exactly who I was.

I got put in a 3-man cell with a homie from New Mexico and a Sureño. We
clicked. It was cool. The guy from New Mexico had been in the room the
longest, so he had seniority. He was a little grumpy, but we got along.

After a while, I got a job as a pod porter. Back to getting that dollar a day so
I could get my soups and hygiene or whatever I needed from commissary.

Yard was mandatory, a rule set by the homies not the institution. We got
an hour a day, alternating mornings one day, evenings the next—two pods
at a time.

I wasn't a morning person. Still wasn't sleeping great. So when I could skip
the morning yard, I did. But I went most days.

The 600 unit shared a fence with 700. That's when I got introduced to a
homie across the fence named Smiley—from Phoenix. I guess he'd been to
state before and had the keys for the AZ Chicano car at the time.

He never had a fondness for me. Got agitated when I stopped showing up
to morning recs. I think they had a conversation about it—but they let it
be.

This was the longest I had ever been incarcerated at that point.

One morning, I woke up. We were locked down. TVs in the dayroom were off. No movement. Kitchen workers didn't even get pulled. Something was different. They didn't tell us anything.

The date was September 11, 2001.

I started listening to the radio. That's when I heard about the planes. The hijackings. The Twin Towers.

I know a lot of people got hurt. People lost loved ones. But I think it's crazy how we're almost amused by catastrophe. How we look forward to seeing destruction.

It didn't directly affect me—except we got locked down for the next couple days.

Life went on. I didn't think much of it. It felt like a TV episode. Like a reality show.

But now, years later, I've had my own losses. And I can respect what those people went through. My condolences to all who lost someone in that.

By this time, I had all the discovery in my case. I saw all the evidence they had against me.

Turns out, they had a whole investigation going—trying to find out who Lazy Huero was. The homie I got the guns from? He was telling it all. But he didn't know my government name.

There was also a confidential informant. Said they'd been to my house on two occasions. Said I was there both times. Even pointed out the car I drove.

Only a couple people knew where I stayed—especially people involved like that. It could only be one of two people: Lil Chino's cousin, locked up with me. Or his brother, who was asleep on the couch when Lil Chino's brother was murdered.

They ran the plates to my S10 Blazer. It came back to my mom. They checked who got mail at that address. They ran all the names.

Then they connected it—because I got pulled over one time with the homie I got the guns from. Another homie got arrested. There was a report.

They took an old booking photo of me to the prison. Showed it to the same homie who gave me the guns. And he identified me as Lazy Huero.

Chapter 40

Even the Closest Ones Will Fold

*betrayal (noun) 1. When someone takes your trust and gives it to the other
side. 2. A silence you thought you earned spoken out loud.*

He didn't pull a gun on me. But he put one in their hands.

I know about the confidential informant now—and I had my suspicions.

I ran into Lil Chino's cousin in the hall and confronted him about it.
I told him, "It had to be you or your brother."

He says, "You think I didn't know your government name? And remember
I came by your house another time in Scarface's car!"

I'm thinking—yeah, that's true. I had already remembered that. I wasn't
sure if he knew my government name or not. But even so, that don't mean
he had to tell the feds all that.

So I tell him, "Then the confidential informant has to be your brother—if
it ain't you."

He's like, "You gotta take that up with him."
Like he had no concern.

I know I would've been offended if someone accused my brother of being
a confidential informant. And if he was? I'd feel a responsibility to handle
it. I'd disown him.

Lil Chino's cousin didn't act troubled. Didn't act disturbed by it at all.
I just kept my distance after that.

Not too long later, he was sentenced. I believe he got 27 months and was sent to a minimum yard in California.

My stepdad had also caught a case after we got raided—after I got arrested.

Come to find out—in my paperwork—it states that while the ATF was raiding the house, he asked to talk to an agent.
He asked them what they were looking for. They told him: machine guns and silencers.

He said he didn't want no trouble. Said, *Jason has always been trouble.* Said he was afraid of me. That I had threatened him with violence before.

But he knew where some guns were being kept—in the bathroom, under the sink, behind the baseboard.
He told them I had shown them to him.

Said he didn't ask me to take them out of the house—because he didn't want to upset me.

He also said there was counterfeit money in the house. That it was mine.

But they found the counterfeit money in *his* stuff. In *his* room. With the original bills and a scanner printer.
And he was trying to throw it on me.

To top it off—he told them where the guns were.
They probably would've never found them. Just like they didn't find that crack.

He snitched.

And yeah—I was the reason why the ATF came to the house. That was my fault. I own that.

I wasn't about to let nobody go down for me. That's why I made sure I told them—*that's my room and that is my bathroom, nobody else uses it.*

I didn't want to kill the guy for what he did.
But I was hurt.

This was the closest thing I had to a dad.
Add all the time together, I'm sure he was only in my life a total of about four years—at most.
But he'd been to prison. Lived a similar lifestyle. I expected more.

And trying to put that counterfeit money on me? Looked real dumb from my perspective.
It was with *his* stuff.
He had the originals.

What a criminal.
No wonder he caught another case.

My mom's always been clean. Doesn't do drugs. Doesn't commit crimes.
I don't know why she was attracted to my stepdad—or any of her boyfriends.

But we can't help who we fall in love with.

Chapter 41

Guilty and Still Breathing

acceptance (noun) 1. When you stop arguing with reality, and start walking with it. 2. The moment you realize surviving is still a kind of victory.

They called me guilty. But I was still alive. And that had to count for something.

I should've known. Even Bam Bam—probably my best friend at the time—said things he shouldn't have said when our apartment got raided.

But I got to give credit to his girl—she held it down. Said she didn't know who I was. Didn't know my name. Didn't know nothing about me.

Ha.
And at that time I was about to be the godfather to their daughter.

It's like that. Expectations will let you down.
Have to accept things for how they are.
And sometimes, people will surprise you.

I wasn't much into watching baseball.
Loved playing it as a kid though.

I remember being in county jail on the juvenile floor, looking out the little window in my cell—watching them build Bank One Ballpark.

I go for all Phoenix and Arizona teams—even if I didn't really follow sports anymore.

My celly from New Mexico was into baseball. He'd been watching the World Series. Diamondbacks were in it.

So I sat down to watch the game.
Everyone did.

I remember—Luis Gonzalez got that hit. Drove in the winning run. It was over.
Arizona finally got a championship.

That was an exciting feeling for me—even if I wasn't into sports anymore. It was pride.

That was where I was from.
The state I was born in.
The city I was raised in.
Where the D-backs played.

We all became champions in that moment.
They represented *us*.

About a week after that—I signed a plea.

Now in the feds, there isn't really a plea bargain. There's no bargaining.

You've got a sentencing guideline chart—criminal history level on top, offense level on the side.

Where they meet? That's your time.

Feds got a 90% conviction rate. They don't need to make deals.
If they pick you up, they've probably already got enough to convict you.

But they will drop a few offense level points if you don't waste their time.

With all the evidence they had on me, the only thing I would've gained by going to trial was maybe—*maybe*—finding out who the confidential informant was.

And even then, maybe not.

Wasn't worth getting more time.

About a week after we locked in the guilty plea, I started getting an idea of what my future looked like.

And then—my 21st birthday came.

I didn't think I'd make it to see 21.
Almost didn't make it to 18.
And if I hadn't gotten picked up by the ATF? I might not have made it to 21.

The way I lived?

Yeah—it was *that* real.

Me and some of the homies made a spread to celebrate.
Made the best of it.
Based on the circumstances.

Chapter 42

Too Much Pride in a Small Space

pride (noun) 1. The thing that helps you stand tall until it keeps you from reaching out. 2. A wall we build so nobody sees how hurt we really are.

It wasn't the system that broke us. It was pride.

I had a couple homies I'd been kicking it with tough.
We were killing time—playing spades, chess, watching TV. Just shooting the shit.

I was closest with Flaco from Mesa and Toby, a Black dude from South Phoenix.

When you find people you really click with while you're locked up, and you're going through that kind of situation, you build a bond.

But it's crazy how easy it is to lose a friendship over nothing.

One day a new guy comes into the pod. He's a character—looks a little funny, acts goofy, cracks jokes. Entertaining for sure.

He'd been there maybe a week or so.

One morning, we get our breakfast trays and sit down. Me and Flaco are at the same table. That new guy is at another.

Flaco's in good spirits, starts joking around a little early.

I don't remember exactly what was said, but he made some joke about that goofy guy being from *my* hood.

I was probably just tired. Took offense to something minor. It didn't mean anything—just a joke.

But me and Flaco almost got into a fight over it.

He was offended that I took offense. I was offended over a dumb joke.

We both let our pride get to us.

After that day, we stopped speaking.

After all the time we spent killing time together—helping each other get through the days—we let one little joke ruin it.

Toby got sentenced not long after. He was being shipped out.
Before he left, he gave me and Flaco all his belongings. Couldn't take it with him.

Toby had tried to get us to be cool again a few times. But we both had too much pride.

And now, without Toby there? I felt alone.

Chapter 43

<u>They Wanted More, but I Took the Win</u>

mercy (noun) 1. When the outcome doesn't match the weight of your past. 2. The moment you realize not everyone wants to see you buried.

They expected time to crush me. But it didn't. I walked out thankful.

After you enter your guilty plea, they have to do a presentence report and make a recommendation. That takes a little time.

I only signed for counts 2 and 3. They dropped the other charges.

My guideline range came out to 37 to 46 months in the Bureau of Prisons.

Every sentence comes with a 3- to 5-year tail of federal probation. My agreement was 3 years—and we stipulated to the low end.

They wanted to add criminal history points because of my juvenile armed robbery. Said it was a serious crime.

They couldn't use the armed robbery on the crack house in the calculations—because I was never convicted. And they didn't like that they couldn't use the drugs they found in the raid against me either. If they had, my offense level would've jumped and I'd be looking at 57 to 71 months.

In the feds, they got prisons all over the country. Different security levels. They even got a supermax underground in Florence, Colorado called the ADX.

Depending on how you're classified—they can send you anywhere.

So we asked that I be kept close to home if possible.

I never asked my mom to come visit me. It was a long drive for her. Visits were behind glass. As long as I got to talk to her on the phone every now and then—I was good.

But I asked her to come visit once—before sentencing. I didn't know where I'd get sent. Or how fast. Or when I'd see her again.

Not long before sentencing she made it to visit. Brought my nephew too. It was good to see them.

February 11, 2002—sentencing day.

I walked in. Saw my mom, I also saw two of the ATF agents. One of them—the one who really seemed to have it out for me.

My public defender was by my side.

I stood before the judge. Gave him my utmost respect and attention.

He gave me my sentence. He committed me to Thirty-seven months in the Federal Bureau of Prisons on counts 2 and 3, to run concurrently.

The courtroom was quiet.

Then a ruckus. Sounded like a door slammed too. It was loud.

I didn't look back. Didn't want to disrespect the judge.

Some people cry when they get sentenced.
Me?
I was full of joy.

I was trying not to smile. I was so happy to only get 37 months.

But that ATF agent? He was pissed. Stormed out of there. Disrespected the judge. Disrespected the whole court.

If it's the United States of America vs. me—he just disrespected the whole country.

The judge also gave me the 3 years probation, a $3,500 fine, and recommended I be placed in an institution in Arizona.

He gave me credit for time served. I had already been locked up about a year.

In the feds, you have to do at least 85% of your sentence. But you can also get up to 6 months halfway house time.

That meant I could be out in another year and a half.

Chapter 44

<u>From Sentenced to Shackled</u>

transition (noun) 1. The space between two chapters where nothing is certain, but everything is in motion. 2. A forced move that tests your mindset more than your body.

I was finally sentenced. But the journey was just getting started.

After I got sentenced, it was like a weight lifted off me.

No more uncertainty. No more not knowing when I might be free.

I had a release date now.
And maybe I'd even get out sooner if I got halfway house time.

Of course, I was counting down the days.
But I was also a little excited to get transferred out of CCA and hit the yard.

It wasn't long. They transferred me and some other sentenced inmates next door to a facility called FCC.
I spent a couple weeks there.

Then early one morning, they got a big group of us.
Shackled us up—just like when we'd go to court.
Put us on buses. Took us to the airport in Phoenix.

It looked just like a movie.
Something like *Con Air* or *U.S. Marshals.*

They had U.S. Marshals posted up with face covers, assault rifles, shotguns.

Snipers on the roof. Inmates chained up. Buses lined up. And a federal airplane.

They don't tell you where you're going.

If you get put on that plane, you're probably going to Oklahoma City—their transfer center.
The plane pulls right up to it.
Otherwise, they've got buses going different places.

I wasn't trying to get put on that plane.

I sat there for a while.
They called a lot of names.

Finally, they called mine.
I got put on a bus.

Once we hit the I-17 going north, it looked like we were headed to Black Canyon.

Just because I got put on the Black Canyon bus didn't mean I'd stay there.
That was the most ideal spot for me—close to home.
But some people on that bus were just holdovers.
They'd catch another bus somewhere else.

We get to R&D—Receiving and Discharge.
That's where I found out.

I was designated to FCI Phoenix, a.k.a. Black Canyon.

Technically a medium, but considered a medium-high.
They put what's called a manageable variable on me.

My custody level points were high.
I should've been sent to a USP.
But I was already under two years to the gate—and there were no USPs in
Arizona at that time.

So I had to stay out of trouble.
Or they'd send me packing.

When I used to hear about federal prison, I imagined a country club.
People playing tennis. Camp Snoopy.

But this wasn't that.

I'll be honest—Maricopa County Jail was the worst place I've been locked
up.
Probably the hardest place to do time because of the conditions.

Might be better now that Sheriff Joe is gone, but that place was inhumane.

I never been to state prison.
But I know a lot of people who have.

Federal?

Has to be worse.

Too many different groups. Too many different races.
Every race had branches. Groups within groups. You had every nationality
you could think of.

Something was always popping off.

Chapter 45

Clearing the Table

closure (noun) 1. When the open loops that haunt your past finally get tied off. 2. The freedom that comes from knowing nothing is hanging over your head anymore.

I didn't go back to finish a fight—I went back to close it.

FCI Phoenix has four different units named after Native tribes: Mohave, Navajo, Pima, and Yuma.

Each unit has an A and B side—except for Yuma. It's considered the orientation unit.

Yuma also has an annex for transfers, the whole unit was separated from the general population.

That's where I was stuck—until they had room to transfer me into one of the other units.

They had plans to close off the annex and open Yuma to the yard.

But who knew when that would actually happen. They said soon though.

I had a probation violation from Maricopa County hanging over my head.

So I filed a writ—wanted to take care of it, get it out the way.

It took some time. But not too long.

Unexpectedly—they let me know I was going to court.

Maricopa County.

There were a few of us going back at the same time.
This white kid named Nate—my age—was also coming from FCI.
We kind of stuck together through processing.
Ended up in Towers jail together. Even in the same pod.

Coming from CCA and FCI to Maricopa County?
Big difference.

It was different scenery. But I was ready to go back by the time I got there.
I couldn't wait to be done with court.

Didn't see too many familiar faces while I was in Towers.
But I did run into Flaco from Mesa.

We were both thrown off seeing each other there.
But it was cool.
We chopped it up like old times. Didn't even bring up that nonsense from CCA.

My court date came.

Public defender pulls me aside.

He says, "Which of your federal charges do you want to plead guilty to for the violation?"

I said, "Pick one. It don't matter."

He said, "Hold up. We'll plead to the silencer. Because in the state—it's not considered a gun. That way, they won't come back and try to give you gun charges later."

I said, "They can do that?"

He said, "Yeah."

So I pled guilty to violating my probation by having a silencer.

They took care of everything that day.
Put in a motion to just reinstate my probation after I got out of the feds—and run it concurrent with my federal probation.

I was hoping I'd get sent back to FCI Phoenix that day.
But it took about another week or two.

Chapter 46

Cool Breeze on the Yard

discernment (noun) 1. The power to see through people without needing to expose them. 2. That quiet strength that knows who's real and who's frontin'.

I didn't need a crew. I had clarity.

I get back to FCI Phoenix, and they got Yuma unit opened up to general population.

So I had more freedom than before.

Things kept getting better.

But I didn't really have anyone I was hanging with tough.

I was kind of an outcast in my car.

There were a lot of AZ guys from Tucson. Not many from Phoenix.

They used to call me *Cool Breeze.*

Like I thought I was too good.

But it wasn't that.

I just didn't have much in common with the other homies.

I probably got along best with a Latin King from Chicago named Nato.

He was my celly for a minute.

We used to argue all the time.

He was always, *Chicago this, Chicago that*—always comparing Chicago to Phoenix.

"No skyscrapers," he'd say. *Ha.*

Had me in the library looking up stats—proving Phoenix was the fifth biggest city in the U.S.

Even though we argued about dumb stuff, we both had that same type of hustle energy.

Out on the mainline now, I'm meeting the homies from other units on the yard.

They had a weight pile.
You had to get in with someone's workout car or just try to get in where you fit in.

I liked to stay outside till last rec call.
Most people went in early.
That gave me an extra 30 minutes—time to get in my own groove on the weight pile.

Smiley from the 700 unit in CCA was there too.

One day I had a little issue with a paisa who worked line service in the kitchen.
I wasn't dumb enough to cause a wreck over it.
So I went to Smiley—thinking he was still the guy to talk to.

He used to be the shot-caller at CCA.
And he was the one trippin' on me for not going to morning rec.

Come to find out—he's nobody here.
Just some fool who's a junkie on the streets.

That right there showed me—
A lot of people ain't who they portray to be.
And if you believe they are, they'll run with it.

Not all people in a position of power are righteous.

Throughout my time incarcerated, I saw people in power come and go.
Some of them loved me like a brother or nephew.
Some of them disliked me for no reason—or maybe their own reasons.

But I was always solid.
True to who I was.
And true to my beliefs.

Chapter 47

<u>College for Criminals</u>

strategy (noun) 1. A smarter way to do the same thing just without getting caught. 2. A plan disguised as patience.

I wasn't thinking about going straight. I was thinking about leveling up.

I got moved to Navajo unit on the A side.
Another 3-man cell.

This time with a homie from Coolidge, AZ named Chino—and a homie from Tucson.

I got a job in the kitchen.
Started off with dishes.

Didn't last long—I didn't like that job.

Moved to floors.
Easy work.

It's not that I'm lazy.
I just look for the easy wins.

In the feds, they have pay grades.
But you can only move up so far without a high school diploma or a GED.

I wanted to get my GED anyway.

I got into school.
I've always been smart. I just needed a little refresh.
I breezed through the classes.

They had three different levels.
I hit the last level in no time.

All I wanted was to take the test.
Next time they did GED testing—I was on the list.

And I guess you could say it's something I'm proud of.

With how little time I actually spent in high school, the way I scored made me feel good about myself.

With the GED, I eventually made it to a Grade 2 pay rate.
I just had to make sure the dining room was clean after evening chow.

Still easy work.
Most of the day, us afternoon kitchen workers just chilled.

I had a homie I really clicked with there.
Cool as hell. Humble. Solid.

He was doing like 30 years.
Went to trial. Got busted for a drug tunnel that ran under the border from Mexico to AZ.

He was trying to get sent to Mexico—where he was also wanted.
And eventually, he did.

I kept in contact.
Sent him a Christmas card every year after I got out.

We used to play a lot of spades. Even rummy.

Sometimes, good people are involved in some crazy things.

I did everything I was supposed to.

Stayed out of trouble.

Kept it real.

I remembered that jail talk when I was 14.

And how the second I got out—I went right back to the streets.

So I wouldn't say I was gonna change.

I'd say—I wasn't tripping on probation.

That's nothing.

I don't get high.

So probation's easy.

I was an even smarter criminal now.

It was like I was at college for criminals.

And while I'm here?

I'm looking for a plug.

Some of the people in there were involved in major dealing.

Bigger than I ever thought of. Associates of individuals such as Pablo Escobar.

My homie was there because of a tunnel you could drive tons of coke through. Not one you crawl through.

I also learned what *conspiracy* was.
You could catch charges for just talking about a deal.
Didn't even need to get caught with drugs.

I learned you could cross the border with under 50 pounds of weed.
And if you had no criminal history, first two times you get caught—you probably just get probation.

That's where my mind was at.

Chapter 48

<u>The Last Block</u>

departure (noun) 1. When you physically leave a place, but emotionally leave a piece of yourself behind. 2. The strange joy of being free mixed with the pain of leaving people who aren't.

I didn't leave in cuffs. I left with stories, scars, and a soul that finally felt light.

The rest of my time just flowed.

I went to work. I worked out.
I saw people come. I saw people go.
I saw people go—and come back again.

The homie from La Victoria even showed up on the yard at one point.
It was good to see him.
I mean—not good he was there.
But if he was gonna be locked up, I was glad we were on the same yard.

Eventually, I had seniority in my cell.
I moved in some younger homies—more my age, more in common.

We had some good times.
Chillin'. Crackin' jokes. Making spreads. Playing the card game *Speed*.

I ended up getting the majority of my tattoos while I was at FCI Phoenix.

Spent the night in my neighbor's cell a couple times while his celly stayed in mine, so we could work on my arm at night.

An AZ homie gave me a 50 paper to give to him for the work—and told me not to worry about paying him back.

That meant a lot to me.

Most people try to keep you in their pocket—make you owe them so they can have power.
This homie? He just did a solid.

I had a paisa from Durango work on my chest piece.
I was trying to finish up some work on my right arm before release—sneaking over to Mohave unit where a homie from Phoenix was working on me.

I haven't had much tattoo work since I've been out.
But I got something planned.

It wasn't a far trip to Black Canyon for my mom—only about 20 minutes from the house.
But I only had her and my sister visit like two, maybe three times the whole time I was there.

Told her I had laundry on Saturdays.

But I called a lot.
Phone calls were only 15 cents a minute locally, and I could buy 300 minutes a month.
So I made a 10-minute call almost every day.

And then—one day—I noticed something.

The days I kept marking off on my calendar kept dwindling down.
Until they were gone.

It's weird how it ends up being kind of sad—leaving prison.

You feel some guilt.
You've built bonds. Brotherhoods.
And now you're walking free while they stay.
Especially when they've got a lot of time.

My release date came.

The night before, my celly threw me a going-away spread.
All the homies in the unit came by to show love.

At the same time it was sad—but it felt good.

The next day, I got called to R&D.

Took a few things—my letters, my paperwork.
Left everything else with my cellys.

And I was out.

I got four months halfway house time.
So technically, I was still property of the Federal BOP.

They don't allow anyone to pick you up.
They have a taxi take you from FCI Phoenix to the halfway house on Roosevelt.

Chapter 49

<u>Out But Not Free Yet</u>

reentry (noun) 1. When freedom comes with conditions, and every step forward feels like a test. 2. The awkward phase between being a prisoner and becoming a man again.

I was out. But I still had to prove I belonged.

Not that I did a long stretch of time.
But maybe my life had gone so fast that when it finally slowed down inside, it felt longer.

It was like when you're driving 80 mph for a while—and suddenly drop down to 40.
Everything feels slow.
Until you balance back out.

That whole cab ride to the halfway house—I was excited.

The halfway house was an apartment complex, but it had staff you had to check in with.
They fed you. Had chow times. Rules.
It was coed too—females stayed there.

They put me in a one-bedroom apartment with three other guys.
One dude had a bed in the living room.
The room had two sets of bunk beds.
I was the new guy. Got one of the top bunks.

Right away, I started job hunting.
Well—*sort of.*

I wasn't really looking for a job at first.
I was just filling out five applications a day—at random places near wherever I wanted to be that day.

I just had to be back by 5 PM.

I did that for two weeks.
Fifty applications. Not one callback.

Even if I wasn't serious at first—that got discouraging.

Since it had been two weeks with no job, I started getting restrictions.
They sent me to talk to the staff worker who helps you look for work.

Still using newspaper classifieds back then.
He gave me a couple numbers to call and told me to hit the jobs resource center downtown.
They had phones, computers—everything.

Next day, I went there.
Called the first number—don't remember what happened.
Then called the second.
A produce company.

A guy answered.

I tried to be professional—asked if they were hiring.

He came back with attitude.
"How'd you get this number?"

I said, "Out the newspaper."

He said, "We didn't put no ad in the paper."

Now I got an attitude too.
I said, "You hire felons or not?"

He said, "Yeah, we hire felons."

We're still talking with attitude.

I said, "What's your name?"

He said, "Juan."

I said, "I'll be on my way."

I went down there.
Didn't think I'd get hired.
Took a while—I was on the bus.

Got there—it was a warehouse in an industrial plaza.
Other warehouses lined the strip.

I walked in.

A short, stocky, bald-headed Chicano pulled up on a pallet jack.

I said, "I'm looking for Juan."

He said, "I'm Juan."

I said, "I talked to you on the phone."

He said, "Oh nah—you must of talked to the manager. He left for the day."

Then he said, "Let me get the supervisor."

Another Chicano showed up—tall, bald—name was Hector.

He took me to the office, gave me an application, and said, "Fill this out and leave it with the office guy."

Next day—I get a call.

They want me to come in for an interview.

Now my attitude's a little different.

Went from ready to go fight to prepping for an interview.

I showed up.

They sent me to a different office—around the corner from the other one.

I walked in.

There's a Mexican guy—short hair, light beard.

Couldn't tell if he was Chicano or paisa.

He says, "Take a seat."

He's holding my application.

Says, "I see you don't have any experience. You got a drivers license?" Then before I could answer, he says "Did I talk to you on the phone?"

I said, "Yeah."

He said, "Do we hire felons?"

Chapter 50

<u>When the Story Paused</u>

wisdom (noun) 1. Not just knowing everything but understanding when you didn't. 2. The stillness that comes after surviving your own fire.

I didn't just live through hell. I listened to what it was trying to tell me.

Everything I had been through to this point—I felt turned me into a man.

I had been through so much, I felt I knew everything.
I didn't break. I survived.
And now I was 23 years old.

I had said before—I wasn't religious.
But I did try to turn to God a couple times.

I even wondered—how does someone sell their soul to the devil?

While I was in prison, I asked God to give me something I could sell like dope—but wasn't dope.
Something legal.

Maybe I could be as good at selling a legal product as I was at selling drugs.
Then I'd never end up in there again.

But honestly—people will literally sell their children for drugs.
There is nothing on this planet like it.

I could never comprehend it.
But I did learn—life takes many people to make the world go round.
And there is a reason for everything—even if it doesn't make sense to me.

I was right, though.
I *did* know everything.

Everything I needed to know *at that point in time*—everything to keep me
going along my path.
To become the man I am today—and the man I'm still becoming.

We reincarnate many times in a single lifetime.

I wasn't a man at 23.
I was still a boy, programmed by gangster rap and movies, led in a direction
of destruction.

To go to hell and back—to be able to tell my story, and change lives!
It was all part of my process.
My life experience.
My learning experience.

I have no regrets.

I have compassion for anyone who may have gotten hurt along the way.
But their pain was part of *their* process too—as it intertwined with mine.
Part of something much bigger.

I never had sympathy for people who got hurt in the game—drug dealing,
gangbanging.
We know what we sign up for.

It took me a while to see—it's the loved ones who suffer.
They're innocent.

And as I see that now—I no longer want to be a part of causing that pain.
Even if I think someone deserves it.

Because I'm still harming *their* family.
Even if not physically.

I've learned to be thankful.
To not take life for granted.

I used to think—when we die, that's it. Just darkness. Game over.
But it's obvious there's so much more.

And life can be amazing—if you just open your eyes to it.

You have to be mindful of what you feed your brain.
What you associate yourself with.
The way you see yourself, and speak about yourself.

I didn't think I'd live to see 21.
But I put that out there.

One of my brother's friends told him when I was a kid—
"Your brother's gonna be one of the hardest gangsters."

So I lived it.

This book isn't meant to glamorize anything.
But I know there are many people who've been through it like I have.

And I believe—if someone as dark as I once was can see light.
Then so can you.

I'm not trying to push religion on anyone. Or spirituality. None of
that.
I'm not against it either.

I believe—whatever makes you a better person, whatever makes you feel better about yourself.

That's what you should go with.

Because when you're ready to learn—the teacher will appear.

PART TWO

Rising From the Ashes

Chapter 51

Energy Vampires and the Rebuild

awareness (noun) 1. The moment you stop just surviving—and start observing. 2. A lightbulb that flickers after years of darkness, showing you what you were really living in.

I didn't break down. I was being rebuilt.

Life had to throw a lot at me to finally break me down far enough that I could rebuild myself mentally.

I have a strong, stubborn soul that just won't quit.

I even took pride in being strong enough mentally to not break after all I'd been through.
I felt like I could go through anything life wanted to throw at me—like, *go ahead. Try it.*

But that mindset was actually stopping the growth.

You can't grow or learn if you feel like you already know everything.
You have to be open-minded.
Willing to see things from a different perspective.

I was stuck on the hamster wheel chasing money my whole life.
Thought, *If it don't make dollars, it don't make sense.*

Had that *hustle all day, I can sleep when I'm dead* mentality.

But sleep is when your body heals itself.
Lack of sleep can make you delusional, irritated easily, unable to think clearly—even see things that aren't there.

Honestly? A tired driver is worse than a drunk driver.
Both are no good—but a drunk driver is slow to react.
You fall asleep at the wheel?
You won't even know it's time to react.

I was tired. Worn out.

Even when I *did* get rest—I still felt tired.
I'd drink energy drinks thinking that was helping.
It wasn't.

That crash afterward?
That was slowing me down even more.

My internal battery felt like the battery in an old phone—loses charge faster now.
Or like something was pulling charge from me.

I don't know why, but I must've heard the term *energy vampire* somewhere.
And that's what I felt was happening.

Something was draining me beyond my will.
It wasn't just physical tiredness.
It was mental too.

I even had a dream one time—someone I know, someone I respect, someone intelligent, came to me.

And in that dream they told me:
Someone's taking your energy from you.

Like I said—when you're ready to learn, the teacher will appear.
And the teacher comes in many forms.

But there's no way my younger self would've taken any of this seriously.
I would've been like: *You crazy. You lost it. Energy vampires? What, you watching Twilight or something?*

No such thing as a vampire, right?

But I looked it up.
And I came across some information that led me down a new path.
A new way of seeing things.
And it taught me how to recharge.

Chapter 52

<u>The Mic Was a Mirror</u>

reflection (noun) 1. A beat that makes you nod your head while your soul rewrites itself. 2. What happens when your art stops lying for you and starts healing you.

I didn't just live through hell. I listened to what it was trying to tell me.

I was tired and burnt out on who I was—on the beliefs I was programmed with through the traumas I survived.

I wanted to lie to myself and say they weren't that bad.
That it was normal.

But I felt like I'd take a step forward, then two steps back.
Like I kept going down dead-end paths.

I had to learn to see that I couldn't keep doing the same thing and expect different results.

Music seemed like my way out.
But it was another program.

I had watched artists escape poverty with music and entertainment.
So I followed the blueprint.

And I've been successful with it—up to a point.

It helped me learn a lot.
It helped me release.

I made music that told my life stories.
But the beats—the frequencies—and the energy I resonated with—
It was all stuff I was actually trying to get away from.

Even though my music was mostly stories of the past,
By creating gangster rap—I kept that energy present.

I still had to watch my back.
And now I was getting known—which made me more of a target.

Jealousy.
Hate.
People watching.

The goal was to get out the hood.
To rise above it.
But gangster rap kept me right there—in it.
Knee deep.

And then I started seeing how fake it all was.

I've heard really good songs—but they were made by some kid who never even stepped foot in the trenches.
Never lived anything close to what they rapped about.
Just taking the authenticity away completely.

Or you'd see a rapper get into trouble—acting like a gangster for the camera—
Then turn around and snitch.

That's against the very programming a gangster is supposed to live by to be respected.

But I had to realize—most listeners aren't gangsters.
So they don't care.

And really—why did *I* care?

Because I survived what they only pretend to rap about.
So I took offense to it.

But maybe I shouldn't have been living that way to begin with.

Music taught me how to tell my story.
But I had to stop letting it tell me who I was.

Chapter 53

<u>Watch What You Feed Your Mind</u>

programming (noun) 1. The silent instructions you absorb from music, media, and environment until they become you. 2. What you don't realize is shaping you until you start to wake up.

Your brain doesn't know the difference between what you watch and what you live.

Have you ever watched a sad movie and you can feel it—like really feel it?
You get teary-eyed. Or sad yourself.

Or listened to a song that hypes you up?
Gets your blood rushing?

I was always in denial—especially when I was younger.
I didn't want to believe what music and television could do to me.
How it could manipulate my energy.
Make me feel a certain way.

We don't want to believe that something we like—or are attracted to—is bad for us.
But I can admit it now.
I see it clearly.

I was even creating songs that could easily be the soundtrack to a murder.

Music can be healing.
But it can also be dangerous.

There are artists that make songs I resonate with—
Songs that trigger old memories and pull my mindset back into a dark place.

I've heard Christian rappers using beats with the same frequency as murder rap—
Talking about taking out the opposition.

And even if they mean the devil,
It still gives off that same violent energy.

Your mind is *very* impressionable at a young age.

I was 8 years old and I knew Eazy-E's *Boyz in the Hood* word for word.
I was listening to Too Short's *Life Is...*
Watching the movie *Colors*.
And I ended up a gangbanging dope dealer.

And I'm not the only one.
How many of us did?

Look at the kids today.
Look at how music influences them.

They'll work hard at a job all week to buy one designer shirt—
Because that's what the rappers wear.

They see guns in videos and pictures—so they pose with guns too.
Kids taking pictures with firearms and posting them on social media like it's a game.
Just trying to be cool.

You watch enough reality shows with toxic relationships,
And you'll start second-guessing your own.

Start thinking your partner is cheating. Or sneaking around.

We're attracted to drama.
We slow down for car crashes.
We binge crime shows, violence, betrayal.

We consume massive amounts of negativity without even realizing it.

But your mind?
It does.

You have to watch what you feed it.

You attract what you give your attention to.

The universe doesn't speak English or any language.
It speaks *emotion*.
Vibration.

And your brain doesn't know the difference between what you watch and
what you live.

Chapter 54

<u>Who Am I Without the Mask?</u>

identity (noun) 1. The person you are when nobody's watching and you're not performing. 2. What's left when you stop trying to prove something to the world.

You don't really know yourself until you take the mask off and sit with what's under it.

I loved traveling and going fishing when I was a kid.
Playing in the creek or riverbed. Climbing trees.

But at some point, I forgot what those things meant to me—
Or how much I enjoyed them.

I was too busy living in the concrete jungle.

I didn't have time for peace.
And honestly, I couldn't comprehend how that could even mix with the life I was living.

It never made sense to me when I'd see homies go tubing, or camping on the weekends.
Then come back and gangbang.

Or work a full-time 9-to-5 job,
then go hit the streets like clockwork.

I used to think—
If they had the discipline to work or go camping and do positive, whole-

some stuff—

Then why gangbang at all?

That wasn't survival. That was image.

I wasn't part-time. I was in it all the way.

Nonstop hustle. Nonstop gangbanging.

But prison changed that.

You have to get along with all the other gangbangers when you're locked up—Even if they're from rival sets.

So why get out, start banging again, and risk going back in
Just to be cool with all of them inside?

It made no sense.

And honestly, I was never heavy on proving my gang was harder than anybody else's.
I was always more like—
This is where I'm from. Don't disrespect me and we're good.

That's still how I move now.

If someone's not in my personal space, threatening me or mine?
I let it go.

You can say whatever you want about me from a distance.

There was a version of me that might've gone off the deep end over it before.
Now? I won't lose sleep.

But as a man, I will always defend myself and my family if I feel there's a threat.

The hustle—it's always been my passion.

I chased money because I thought it represented freedom.
But it enslaved me.

I was fooled.
Like the carrot and the stick.

I lost a lot of time—
Time with family, time just enjoying life—because I was always chasing.

And what happens when you chase something?
It runs from you.

I didn't realize it at the time, but I had always been attracting money.
I just didn't know it.

You gotta let it flow to you.

If you feel scarcity—if you move like you don't have enough—
The universe picks up on that.
It goes with that energy.

Even the small things matter.

I ask the universe to bless me with abundance.

So if I see a penny on the ground?
I pick it up.
And I say thank you for all I have, and all I shall receive.

Chapter 55

<u>Living in Alignment</u>

alignment (noun) 1. When your thoughts, actions, and spirit finally stop arguing. 2. That feeling when you're not chasing peace because you've become it.

I stopped forcing everything. I started flowing with life instead of fighting it.

I stopped trying to swim against the current and started going with the flow.
You can't force a square peg into a round hole.

There are things I've learned in this life that I can't change.
Things I have no control over.

It's my choice whether I let those things upset me—or just accept them.

I was programmed to be prideful in ways that kept me from growing.
I had to learn: it's okay to ask for help.
It's okay to make mistakes.

Sometimes you need those mistakes
So you can learn the lesson you couldn't hear before.

I learned to own my faults.
Own my wrongs.

That one was hard.
But when you dissolve your ego—or even just put it in check—
It gets easier.

I know I'm not perfect.
But that doesn't mean I shouldn't try my best.

There's no one right way.
Everyone is right in their own mind.

I had to learn to stop giving uninvited opinions.
Some things aren't meant to be said—or aren't ready to be heard.

I've learned to pick and choose my battles.
To protect my energy.

That's one of the things that's helped me the most.

I stopped taking things for granted.
I appreciate the small things.

I cut off what doesn't serve me.
That's not selfish—that's self-preservation.

Protecting your energy is everything.

And when you start practicing these things?
You feel lighter.
Not heavy.
Not weighed down.

Try walking around with a smile.
Find reasons to be happy—not reasons to be mad.

Learn to love yourself.
Love who you are.
Be comfortable in your own skin.

Because health is wealth.

And mental and physical health?

They go hand in hand.

Chapter 56

<u>What You Speak, You Create</u>

vibration (noun) 1. The unseen frequency your thoughts and words carry into the world. 2. What you call in—whether you meant to or not.

Speak life. Or stay silent.

Words are powerful. They say it's called *spelling* because you cast spells with words.

I don't know how true that is—but I'm open-minded to it.

What I do know is this:
If you put enough energy into the words you speak, you can manifest things.

And those things don't always materialize how you expect.
That's why they say—*be careful what you wish for.*

I remember asking God to give me something I could sell like dope that *wasn't* dope.
And the universe answered.
More than once.

I had a t-shirt hustle.
And I ran it like a corner boy team selling crack.

I ended up with a hot dog cart.
Same thing—it became the new dope spot, just legal.

I've had CDs.

Concert tickets.

And I moved them the same way.

Fast. Hustle. Distribution.

I asked for a million dollars once.

And I got offered an opportunity to move to Mississippi,

Run a store 7 days a week from 10 a.m. to 7 p.m.

I was told I'd be a millionaire in a year.

But I declined.

Because that's not what I want to do.

That's not my passion.

And when you do something in life that isn't your passion—

You're just a modern-day slave.

Look at Tupac.

He rapped about death often.

Even made a song called *Death Around the Corner.*

And he passed young.

Snoop Dogg made a song called *Murder Was the Case.*

Then he had to fight a real-life murder case.

Coincidence? Maybe.

But maybe not. I don't believe in those.

When you speak darkness over your life long enough,

The universe starts to believe you.

And more importantly—*you* start to believe you.

If you speak about yourself with love, power, and purpose?
You become that.

If you speak about yourself like you're doomed, broke, cursed?
That's what you become too.

I try to speak life now.

I look at myself in the mirror—and I look for greatness.
Because if I don't see it in me first,
The world never will.

Chapter 57

Discipline Over Motivation

discipline (noun) 1. Doing what's necessary long after the hype wears off. 2. The quiet force behind every transformation.

*Motivation feels good. Discipline *does* good.*

I had to start being more self-disciplined—
And create good habits.
I had to let go of the bad ones.

One of the first changes I made was with my diet.
You are what you eat.

You can't put cheap gas into a BMW and expect it to run efficiently—So why would I do that to my body?

I had to learn that food is fuel.
So I started eating things that made me feel good *after* I ate them.
Foods that gave me energy.
Not food that made me feel slow and tired.

Fruits. Vegetables. Clean fuel.

Pizza, soda, cakes, ice cream—I had to cut them out.

Now I drink mostly water—And not much else.

I started eating better and I started feeling better.
Then I got more disciplined about exercise.

Moving my body.
Going to the gym.

Physical health leads to better mental health.
You start to feel better about how you look—
Your confidence builds.

It's a domino effect.
It all goes hand in hand.

I also made sleep a priority.

I used to think I could grind all day and sleep when I'm dead.
But sleep is when your body regenerates.
You *need* it if you want to be sharp.

And I got more mindful about what I fed my brain.
Like I said before—watch what your mind consumes.

Guard your peace.
Reject negative thoughts.
Banish them when they try to creep in.

And most importantly—Don't live in the past.

You can't change it. So I stopped obsessing over it.
I just keep moving forward.

Because that's what discipline does.
It carries you when motivation disappears.

Chapter 58

Guarding the Mission

focus (noun) 1. The discipline to keep your energy where it matters. 2. What you protect when you know your future is sacred.

Not everyone is meant to ride with you. Some people are just a detour.

Not everyone is meant to come along for the ride. I've asked the universe to remove those who need to be removed—

So I can continue on my path to becoming the greatest version of myself.

And sometimes, people just fall off out of nowhere.

It's not always bad blood.

It's just different paths.

Different levels.

This isn't about thinking I'm too good.

It's about understanding something real:

The hood don't love you.

Look what happened to Nipsey Hussle—in his own hood.

People want to see you do good—

But not better than *them*.

If you've got more drive, more self-discipline, more hustle—

And you start leveling up?

Some people get jealous.

Some pray on your downfall.

You think people want to see you rise out of poverty—
While they're still stuck there with no plan?

Misery loves company.
And that energy can cost you everything.

All money ain't good money.
Watch what you say yes to.

Some bags aren't worth the headache—
Or what's attached to them.

You can't save everyone.
Some people don't *want* to be saved.

There are folks out there homeless by choice.
Not because they're helpless—
But because they've given up.

Be selective about who gets your time.
Who gets your energy.

We're only given so much time here—
And it's more valuable than gold.

Know your worth.

Because every time you say yes to someone who doesn't value you,
You're saying no to your own growth.

You devalue yourself
When you're accessible to everyone and everything.

You can't spread yourself too thin.

Stay disciplined.

Stay focused.

And most of all—

Guard the mission.

Chapter 59

<u>From Surviving to Serving</u>

purpose (noun) 1. The reason you're still here after everything tried to take you out. 2. When your story becomes someone else's survival guide.

This ain't about fame. It's about fuel.

I used to want a way out.
Of course fame feels good. It strokes the ego.
But deep down, I just love creating—
Music.
Movies.
Content.
That's my real joy.

There were plenty of times I wanted to quit.
I felt like what I was doing wasn't successful enough.

But almost every time I thought about giving up, someone would reach out—
A supporter. A fan.
And say how something I did motivated them
Or helped them get through a dark time.

And that would keep me going.

These days, with the internet, it's easy to get hit with negativity.
Trolls got too much time on their hands,
And they use it to try to disrupt people's peace like it's a game.

That alone detours a lot of people.

Plus, with technology and platforms like TikTok,
It feels like everybody is a rapper now.
Everybody feels famous.

Authenticity? Don't matter to everyone.
Quality? Sometimes it don't even register.

But here's the thing—
There's an audience for everybody.
You just have to find yours.

I don't dwell on likes or views or followers—
But I do understand they matter.
They're currency.
Not dopamine.

Attention is currency.
It means I'm reaching people.

I remember being in Burbank, CA, filming content for a big YouTube
channel.
On a day off, I walked to the gym—figured it'd be my cardio.

Night before that, a cop stopped and harassed me on my way to get
food.
It felt like it was about to get physical—
Until someone at a nearby park caught his attention and was a wit-
ness.
That presence saved me from what could've been another incident.

The next day, I saw cops again.
My instincts kicked in.
I hit record on my phone.

The female cop said it straight up—
They stopped me because of my tattoos.

I didn't even have a TikTok account then,
But about a year later I posted that video.

It went viral.
News channels picked it up.
Lawyers reached out.
One said it was a $5 million lawsuit—
A slam dunk because of the video.

For a moment, I thought—
This is it.

After all those years grinding—
Music, drugs, content, hustle—
This two-minute clip was about to change my whole life.

I started planning.
Give my kids half a million each.
My mom too.
Keep a million to invest.
Start something that gives back.
Create passive income.
Offer services for free.

But then something strange happened.
I felt empty.

Like—*game over. You won.*
But I didn't feel like a winner.

A few weeks later, the lawyer said they were backing out.
No injury. No case.

And just like that—it was gone.

I wasn't shattered.
Disappointed? A little. Low key even was kind of like I'm glad , the hustle isn't over.

But I've learned not to get my hopes too high.
I've been let down too many times.
And I know that programming affects my ability to manifest fully.

But I always feel big success at my fingertips.

I just know now I haven't been fully ready.

There was more to learn.
The journey's not done.
I'm not at the finish line yet.
And that's okay.

Not too many years back, I was making a lot of money—
And had I been *too* blessed at that time, with the mindset I had?

I was too dangerous.

Money ain't evil.
But what people will do for it?
That's the problem.

If I had it all then—with the way I was thinking—
I could've had anybody do anything.
I could've had somebody killed just for disrespecting me.

That ain't power.
That's poison.

I have a higher purpose.
I have a calling.

And every time I stray from it—
Even when I go on side quests—
Life pulls me back to the path.

Sometimes it's gentle.
Sometimes it's not.

But I know now—
I'm not just here to survive.
I'm here to serve.

Chapter 60

<u>What I Know Now</u>

wisdom (noun) 1. Knowledge filtered through pain, patience, and lived experience. 2. Truth that doesn't need to shout to be heard.

You don't have to know everything. Just enough to grow.

Your wants always change. We think we want something.
Then we get it.
Then we want something more—or something different.

And that's okay. That's how you grow.
It helps you set goals—
And then set new ones.

At one point I just told the universe—
I want a house, a good car, and to live comfortably. I didn't even realize
when it happened.
I had already manifested it.
But by the time it came,
I already wanted more.

I used to think being a man meant being feared.
That I had to prove myself.
Show people how violent I could be.
Prove I was willing to take things beyond what most would.

I had beef with a crew once—they came to my house broke my back window of my car.

I was watching TV. Didn't even hear it happen.

I was heated.
They should've just knocked on the door—we could've handled it.

Instead they broke my window and left. When I found out, I grabbed my crew—
And we went and broke as many windows as we could.
Didn't care who it hurt.
Mothers. Grandmothers. Baby mamas.

I didn't care.
Retaliation was a must.

And yeah—it worked.
They never came back.

But looking back?
I was excessive.

That whole beef?
It was a blessing in disguise.

It removed people from my life who didn't serve me.
And it pushed me closer to my purpose.

These days?
Every time I take a shower in my own home—
I think of freedom.
Real freedom.

Because I remember cold showers in jail.

Broken shower heads.

No privacy.

No peace.

Or the birdbaths you take when that's your only option.

Now?

A hot shower is a spiritual experience.

That water hits the top of my head and runs down my face—

It's a reset.

I meditate.

I think.

I create.

I walk out better than I went in.

That's not just hygiene.

That's healing.

Freedom is being able to choose.

And I've always had choices—

Even when I pretended I didn't.

I chose the rocky road.

I chose the long way.

But all those lessons?

They were necessary.

And I'm grateful.

Money can give you freedom—
But it can also enslave you.

You get a good-paying job—
But work long hours, commute far, and have no time to enjoy what you earn.

That ain't freedom.

Work ten years just to earn a 30 day vacation?
That math don't work to me.

Celebrate the small wins.
That's something I've struggled with.

I've done things most people only dream of—
And still didn't give myself the credit.

I've had people around me accomplish great things—
And I didn't always show love,
Because my standards are so high.

But I get it now.

Small wins matter.
They stack.

And having a winning mindset—
That's healthy.

Because life ain't one big win.
It's a series of small ones
That teach you what really matters.

That's what I know now.

I used to chase the world.
Now I just celebrate the moments.

Chapter 61

<u>The Way I Lead Now</u>

leadership (noun) 1. The energy people feel from how you live not what you say. 2. The quiet consistency that leaves no need to explain yourself.

Some people talk power. Others walk peace.

I don't like the term *a real man does this* or *a real man acts like that.*
That's manipulation.
That's programming—meant to make people conform to an image that might not even be healthy.

What's a real man?
That's open for interpretation.

To me?
A man is someone who keeps learning.
Who stays true to his beliefs.
Who improves over time.
And who walks his path no matter how rough it gets. And takes care of what he needs to.

Life requires balance.
Masculine energy.
Feminine energy.
Leaders of all types.

What matters is you keep becoming the best version of yourself.
Energy never stops vibrating—
And neither should we.

Real power?
That's self-control.
That's not letting others pull your strings just to see you react.
It's knowing your value and not needing to prove it.
It's being confident, not arrogant.
Capable of destruction—but choosing peace.

You ever been around someone and just *felt* their presence?
That's energy.

And when your mind isn't cluttered, you can actually *feel* that stuff.
Pick up on it.
Move with it.

The clearer your mind, the more intuitive you become.

I don't preach to people.
I let them observe.
I drop little messages—through music, through what I share online.

Some people don't get it.
They're not there yet.
And that's okay.

Some try to clown it—because they're stuck in a low frequency.

I used to get triggered if someone tried to clown me or something I did.

Back then, it felt like if I didn't react, I looked weak.
Now? I see *not* reacting as strength.

Keeping my composure?
That's power.

I know when someone's not on my level—
And all they're trying to do is bring me down to theirs.

Not long ago, I ran into a situation that made this crystal clear.
There was a guy I used to have issues with.
We never really settled it.
I believe he still holds a grudge.
Probably jealous of how far I've come.

One day, I crossed paths with a woman I didn't know.
Turns out, she was his ex.
She recognized me immediately starts talking to me, she even asked,
"Did he really tie you up?"

I just laughed.
"No," I said.

The old me would've lost it.
Angry that someone lied on me, tried to make me look weak. Ready to
prove myself all over again.

Now? I know better. That lie didn't damage me.
It made me more interesting to her—
And probably to others.

The people trying to tear you down
Are usually the ones still stuck in the past
While you're too busy building a future.

I remember when I used to listen to Nipsey Hussle.
Then his music changed.
And at first, I wasn't feeling it.

But during COVID, I went back.
I was getting in shape.
I put on some old Nipsey while I worked out—
And this time?
It hit different.

I was finally on the frequency he had been on.

That's the power of evolution. The message stays the same.
I question things.
I watch how people move.
And anything I say behind someone's back—
I'll say it to their face.

But I also know—
Not everyone needs to know everything.
Not every good deed needs to be seen.

When it's from the heart,
It's not for clout—
It's for peace.

The real flex is consistency.
Keep going.
That's the key.

Don't let anyone kill your dream.
But also be real with yourself.
What's the *real* dream?
Why are you chasing it?

There was a point I had to sit back and ask myself:
Is it about money?
Is it fame?
Do I want to be a big artist?
A movie star?
An influencer? Truth is—my dreams changed.

There was a time I just wanted to be a rich gangster.
Now?

Now I see grown men throwing up gang signs at 50—
And it feels cringe.

That's not growth.
That's being stuck in a program that doesn't serve you anymore.

My dream now? To travel.
To see new things. Try new food.
Learn new cultures.
To live.
To love.
To raise my family with peace.

To spread knowledge.
To break the chains we were all handed—
And show others they can too.

Because freedom doesn't come in a pill.
It comes when you finally stop running
And start *building*.

And that's how I lead now.

Chapter 62

The Voice in My Head

self-talk (noun) 1. The conversation you have with yourself when nobody else is listening. 2. The silent battle between who you were and who you're becoming.

If you want to change your life, change the way you speak to yourself first.

I am my own worst enemy and my own worst critic. I argue with myself. Constant inner battles.

Matter of fact, I wrote the first line of this chapter then went to the store. On the way, I found a flash drive in the console—forgot it was even in there. Plugged it in. Started skipping through tracks. Landed on a song I recorded a couple years ago. Played it.

It hit hard. The beat was dope. My verse? Solid. Then the featured artist came in—killed it. I pulled into my parking space and let the song finish before I even turned off the car.

There wasn't nothing wrong with that track. Except the frequency. The energy it gave off—I could feel it.

Didn't pay it much mind. Went into the store. Grabbed what I needed. Came back. Got in the car. And the next thing that came on?

A beat I never recorded to. It was hard, too. Had my head noddin. Lyrics started coming to me.

And I caught myself.

Part of me wanted to write to that beat. I even tried to sell it to myself: *Well I could use it in a movie or something.*

But then I thought—this is like a relapse. Because even THINKING of those lyrics—the energy behind it—it was triggering something.

All it would take is the wrong situation, while I'm vibing on that frequency—and boom. One bad decision. Back behind bars. Everything gone.

So I shut it off. I moved on to something with a higher vibration. Something more uplifting.

And you know what? There ain't a lot of that out there anymore.

What happened to the cheerful music? Where's the soul, the joy, the bounce—like those solid gold oldies or rockabilly vibes?

You ever wonder why they took that away?

The truth is, I doubt myself a lot. I doubt my creativity. My value.

I have to remind myself of my accomplishments. Speak life back into myself. Take risks—smart ones. Don't overthink everything—that's always been one of my struggles.

But now?

I watch what I feed my mind. The music I consume. What I watch on TV. What I scroll past on social. Even what I eat.

Throw in a little meditation.

And it all helps me be proud of the man in the mirror.

That matters.

Because when you're at peace with him—you can start rewriting the story. You can control the narrative.

I even have a personal mantra I try to repeat when I wake up and before I go to sleep.

That's my reprogramming.

I don't put myself down anymore. I love myself now. Fully.

Even at 44, I'm proud. Grateful. Blessed.

Some people feel ashamed of their age—I see it as fuel. I'm just getting started. Halfway up the mountain.

So many blessings still to come.

Chapter 63

<u>Learning to Just Be</u>

presence (noun) 1. The stillness that comes when you stop needing to chase, prove, or fix. 2. The ability to be fully in the now without guilt, fear, or distraction.

Sometimes peace isn't found. It's remembered.

The wheels in my head were always turning. Plotting. Planning. Hustling. Trying to figure out the next play, the next move. How to get ahead. How to stay alive.

My mind was a racetrack, and I was burning rubber on every lap. I thought if I wasn't on to the next move, I was falling behind. Because the world don't stop. Bills don't stop. They just pile up. So I kept moving fast.

But what I didn't realize was I was neglecting myself. I never allowed the healing I truly needed.

It wasn't until I slowed down that I started noticing something about myself—and about life.

I've always been drawn to water. The ocean. Creeks. Waterfalls. Rivers. Didn't know why. Just felt something.

There was a time I hadn't been near water for over a decade—from about 12 to 23. But after that? Every time I made my way back to the ocean, or any natural water source—I felt different.

At first, my mind wouldn't stop racing. Even standing on the beach, I was still mentally hustling.

But I kept going back.

And each time, the noise got quieter.

Especially when I was surrounded by nature.

Out there, the air felt different. Lighter. The flowers smelled stronger. The pine trees, too.

The old version of me could care less about the smell of a pine tree. The only tree I was worried about was a money tree.

The mist of the ocean hitting my face. The sound of birds. Seagulls. Something about it all made the chaos in my head slow down.

And then, eventually—silence.

Not the scary kind.
The healing kind.

I learned to just be. No plotting. No rushing. No reacting. Just breathing.

Sometimes I'd take off my shoes and press my feet to the earth. Let it all go. Just let it go.

Because stillness doesn't mean weakness. Stillness is power under control. It's peace by choice.

And in a world that constantly screams for your attention—learning to just *be* is the most gangster thing you can do.

Chapter 64

<u>Why I'm Still Here</u>

purpose (noun) 1. The reason you survived what should've destroyed you. 2. The work your soul came here to complete.

You weren't just saved. You were sent back with a mission.

I don't believe in coincidences. Everything aligns for a reason. Things don't make sense in the moment—but when you zoom out, when you survive it, when you grow through it—then the picture starts to form.

And me?
I'm still here for a reason.

I was meant to be born to my mother and father no matter how that story looked.
It had to be them.

I was meant to touch the lives of every person I've crossed paths with—
Even if just for a moment.

I was meant to create music that reaches the ones who need it.
To write stories that make people feel like they aren't alone.
To build movies that remind others they're allowed to dream bigger.

I'm here to show people that the world is huge—
And they don't have to stay stuck in a small town or trapped in a big city.

I'm here so my children could be born.
So they can walk their own path
And touch the people they were sent here for.

I'm here to show that change is real.
That growth is possible.
That broken doesn't mean finished.

I'm here to give people hope.
I'm here to teach.
To drop seeds through these words—
More powerful than any song I could ever make.

I'm here to tell my story.
I'm here to inspire.
To prove that you can fall, break, burn—
And still come back stronger.

Because I am a Phoenix.
And I didn't just rise from the ashes of hell—
I was *reborn* from them.

And now?
Now I leave a legacy.

Not as the villain.
But as the one who made it out—
And turned back to light the way.

Chapter 65

<u>Walking in Purpose</u>

discipline (noun) 1. The daily decision to honor your growth, even when nobody is watching. 2. A form of self-love disguised as structure.

Purpose doesn't work unless you do.

I'm far from being some holy roller. I'm not a spiritual guru. I'm not religious. But I respect all religions the same.
And I've taken the teachings I resonate with from different faiths, different cultures—
And applied them in my own way.

That's what walking in purpose looks like for me.
It's personal. It's practical.
It's not about being perfect.
It's about being better.

Every day I wake up, I'm still learning.
Still working on myself.
Still trying to stay as disciplined as I can be.

I stay humble.
I stay grounded no matter how blessed I am.

I try to keep a good sleep schedule.
I get that early sun on my body when I rise.
I say my mantras. I give my thanks.

I spend time with my loved ones.
I handle my responsibilities.

I go to the gym. I fuel my body with better choices.
I make time to seek knowledge.
I carve out moments for myself,
And I make time to give and serve others too.

Because I believe we weren't put here to suffer—
Unless there's something we're meant to learn from it.

Now, I'll be real—
Some things I've seen people go through,
I don't believe they had to happen. But they do.
And I don't have all the answers.
I never will.

What I do know is this:
I have to check myself daily. I don't let things trigger me the way they used to.
Because it feels better to help people than to hurt them. But that doesn't mean every day is perfect. I still have days where I feel depression creeping in. Other days I feel like I'm on top of the world. That's just life.

We're chemical beings—dopamine rises and falls.
It's the same reason people feel highs during excitement,
And lows afterward. Like a natural comedown.

When I feel that drop, I don't panic.
I get rest. I breathe. I refocus.
And I do something that lifts me.

My circle got smaller.
I've lost a lot of people over the years.
But I've also traveled and met people that reminded me how good this life
can be.

I stopped just existing.
I live now. Fully.

I've got plans to make it to 120 years old.
So I don't have time to waste.

Walking in purpose?
It's not a one-day thing.
It's not a destination.
It's a lifelong practice.

And I'm still walking.

I don't have it all figured out—
But I wake up every day
And walk it out anyway.

Chapter 66

<u>The Phoenix in Me</u>

phoenix (noun) 1. A symbol of death, transformation, and rebirth rising from ashes, stronger than before. 2. A reminder that your past doesn't define you. It refines you.

You're not just alive. You were reborn for a reason.

The Phoenix is more than just a myth to me.

It's symbolic.
It's spiritual.
It's survival.

It represents rebirth.
Renewal.
A second chance.

It gives hope.
It gives motivation.

Everything the Phoenix stands for—
That's what I had to become.

And the truth is:
Just like the Phoenix is in me—
It's in you too.

I ain't special because I was born in a city named Phoenix.
That's just alignment.

What matters is I rose.

From ashes.

From mistakes.

From near-death.

From darkness.

I have no regrets.

I'm not ashamed of who I was.

I may not be proud of everything I did—

But I am proud of who I became because of it.

That's the difference.

This isn't the end of my story.

It's just a new beginning.

Where legacy means more than lifestyle.

Where ego gets dissolved and turned into purpose—

Like alchemy.

That's what this book is.

That's what this chapter is.

That's what this whole life has been preparing me for.

This is my higher purpose:

To reach you.

To remind you.

To show you that if *I* could rise—

So can you.

You are here for a reason.
You always were.
You just forgot for a while.

So let this be your reminder:

The Phoenix is in you too.

Final Words

From One Phoenix to Another

If you made it this far, thank you. That means you walked with me through the fire, through the ashes, and through the rise.

This wasn't easy for me to write. Some of these pages brought back pain I had buried I didn't even know I had. But they also reminded me just how far I've come. This story isn't about being perfect. It's about being real. About being broken and still moving forward. About the power in not giving up when you had every reason to.

I didn't write this book to glorify the struggle — I wrote it to expose it. To help someone else avoid the traps. To remind you that pain can be turned into purpose. That trauma doesn't get the last word unless you let it. That your past does not have to be your future.

And if nobody told you this before: you matter. You were never meant to stay stuck. The fact that you're still here means your story ain't over. There's a reason you picked up this book. Maybe it was more than curiosity — maybe it was alignment.

I used to think my legacy would be the dirt I did in the streets. Now I know it's the light I leave behind. If you're going through it right now — keep going. If you're still in the fire, don't give up. **You are the phoenix too.** And if this book lit something in you... don't let that flame die. Keep rising.

— J. De Ross

Acknowledgements

I want to thank everyone who believed in me, even when the world only saw the worst in me. If you ever looked past my flaws and saw the good — thank you. Your faith stayed with me.

To the ones who tried to drain my energy, break my spirit, or play me small... I see now that you were part of the path too. You helped shape my direction. Some people push you forward by not walking with you — and I'm no longer mad about it. I'm grateful.

To my uncle and my grandmother — your presence, your energy, your love... I carry it with me.

To my mom — I know I put you through hell, and still, you loved me through it. You never gave up on me. You deserve peace, joy, and everything I couldn't give you back then. This book is proof I heard you — even when I wasn't listening.

Thank you all. The real ones, the lessons, the losses, and the light.

— **J. De Ross**

P.S.

To my Higher Self — thank you for the quiet guidance when I was too loud to listen.

For pulling me through the darkness, even when I thought I was leading myself.

You were always there. I just had to rise high enough to meet you.

About the author

J. De Ross, also known as Lazy Dubb, is a recording artist, actor, and entrepreneur based in Phoenix, Arizona. Once deep in the streets, J. turned his pain into purpose — using his story to inspire others through music, film, and now this book.

Follow him at:
Tiktok @LazyDubb48 | IG: @LazyDubb | YouTube: Lazy Dubb | Website: www.lazyubb.com